Joy of Retirement

Live, Love, and Learn

JOY NEVIN

WATAGE PUBLISHING

ISBN: 978-0-9906-3431-7 (sc)
ISBN: 978-1-4834-4078-1 (e)

WAT-AGE Publishing LLC
1158 Fifth Avenue, Suite 12D, New York, NY 10029
917-584-2931
WAT-AGE Publishing LLC

Because of the dynamic nature of the Internet, any web addresses or links contained in
this book may have changed since publication and may no longer be valid. The views
expressed in this work are solely those of the author and do not necessarily reflect the
views of the publisher, and the publisher hereby disclaims any responsibility for them.

WAT-AGE Publishing LLC rev. date: 11/19/2015

Table of Contents

Dedication vii
The Joy of Retirement: Live, Love and Learn 1
Adjusting to Retirement 7
Learning to Live Together Again, 24/7 17
Choosing Where to Live - Stay Put, Relocate, or Downsize 25
Coping with Even Older Parents and Returning Chicks 35
Looking Your Best - Most of the Time 43
Advantages of Retirement with Time to Travel 57
Reaching Out and Away from Ourselves.................................... 65
Where-With-All Versus Have-It-All 75
Pushing Versus Pulling: Are We Receptive to Change? 83
Challenging Health Crises: Unexpected Claps of Thunder 89
Managing Our Emotional IQ in Older Age................................. 99
Dating in the Elder Years 111
Sex: The Elephant in the Room... 119
Anniversaries: Celebrating and Contemplating............................ 129
Duct Tape....aka...Hushing Mama! 135
Sharing Precious Friendships.. 145
Living the Cup Half Full Life 159
Acknowledgements 171

$\mathcal{D}$εdication

To Dr. Linda Costanzo, whose gentle patience, astute perceptions, and constant support have been the motivating forces in the evolution of this effort. She is the consummate teacher, not only of medicine, but also of the world around her. How blessed I am to have her as a dear friend and mentor. Thank you, Linda, with all my heart. I have loved this journey inspired by you.

And, of course, my heart is forever dedicated to John, my beloved husband of the last fifty-eight years and for the rest of our lives.

"Marriage is more than your love for each other. It has a higher dignity and power, for it is God's holy ordinance through which He wills to perpetuate the human race till the end of time. In your love you see only your two selves in the world, but in marriage you are a link in the chain of generations, which God causes to come and to pass away to His glory and calls into His kingdom. In your love you see only the heaven of your happiness but in marriage you are placed at a post of responsibility toward the world of mankind. Your love is your own private possession, but marriage is more than something personal…it is a status, an office. Just as it is the crown, and not merely our love for each other, that joins you together in the sight of God and man."

Letters and Papers from Prison......Dietrich Bonhoeffer

The Joy of Retirement: Live, Love and Learn

Being seventy-seven years old and writing a book is hardly the norm. Most people do their serious writing decades earlier. Most successful people are reaping the rewards of their writing at this age, basking on a beach in some secluded haven. But a few of us "late bloomers" feel we have much to say without the luxury of time ahead to do it. So, we gather our wits, plunge in, and strive to become interesting and worthwhile writers. We must be disciplined, diligent and determined. In some minds, we "seniors" have drifted into the "expendable" category, so we must try harder to resonate with our readers. I will attempt to do just that.

Ever since my husband left corporate life seventeen years ago, retirement has become a fascinating topic for me. It is a unique condition of being. As more and more baby boomers face their retirement years, the demographic of retirees mushrooms. Many people are retiring earlier than a decade ago, and many are also living longer than ever before. I believe I have learned much of value to share; I would love to help others who are transitioning into retirement, at any phase. I want to share some thoughts about our experience, lessons we have learned, as well as meaningful stories of people we know who have enriched and nurtured us. I believe in my heart that the more we give of ourselves with our knowledge and our experiences, the better we serve others. I have realized, too, that we all bring with us our own backgrounds. We are now more than one generation of retirees. There are those of us who were raised during and shortly after the Great Depression.

We offer one dimension. Those who are baby boomers bring another. We all have different experiences and histories. There are even those retirees who fought in World War II. I believe, however, that the retirement era of life blends us and blurs our age factor. Our common threads will weave us together. Retirement has many phases. Children also need to know what their parents are feeling, what they are experiencing. Knowledge breeds wisdom, and wisdom breeds understanding. Retirement is a time of jolts and joys. It can also be the happiest time of our lives.

I invite each reader to sit back and embrace the thoughts expressed in this book. But first, allow me to share some brief insights into my earliest years. What a pivotal time of life! Childhood is the springboard to adulthood. A caption under an email photo I once received said: *"Babies are such a nice way to start people!"*

I was a post-Depression baby, born in early 1938, on the eve of Hitler's invasion of Czechoslovakia. Thanks to President Franklin D. Roosevelt and his WPA, the American economy was stabilizing, people were struggling out of the Great Depression, and slowly rebuilding their shattered lives. At this same time, Europeans were feeling the effects of the Third Reich. The vicious vendetta against political dissidents and the Jewish population had begun. In early 1939, Nazis marched into Poland, signaling the beginning of World War II. The brutality of Hitler's sub-human treatment of European Jews knew no limits. The hideous embers of the Holocaust were kindled and ignited.

But in Shaker Heights, Ohio, as the daughter of a handsome young lawyer and his bright, beautiful wife with her lovely almond shaped eyes and delicate, competent hands, I was dearly loved and blissfully protected from world events. My parents welcomed my birth, as did my sole sibling who to this day says I was an "answer to her prayers." At age six, she did not want to be an only child. After a difficult pregnancy and birth, my mother patiently coped with a newborn afflicted with pyloric stenosis, or projectile vomiting. Luckily, by the late thirties, doctors discovered syrup of paregoric soothed this condition, and I thrived.

One of my first memories is the impact of World War II on my family. I remember my father walking with me along our street, lined on both sides with tall arching elms, and pointing to little flags in the windows.

If a flag had a blue star it meant that a son was in the military. If the flag's star was gold, then we knew that the family member had died in battle. I remember crouching in my parents' darkened bedroom during air raid drills. I remember the day my mother dropped a sack of sugar. It scattered to all corners of the room. With tears streaming down her face, she crumpled onto the kitchen floor and tried to scoop up whatever confection she could salvage to bake my dad's birthday cake. Rationing was real. Commodities like gasoline, butter, sugar, and nylon stockings were scarce and precious. However, from a child's point of view, life felt safe. My parents worked hard to create as much normalcy as possible. Sunny days in winter meant tobogganing with my dad and sister. Christmas mornings were magical. We could walk to school with playmates, hang upside down on parallel bars during recess, and play hopscotch after coming home. Spring and summer offered softball practice in the street and giggling games of hide and seek with neighbor children. And until the polio scare struck in the mid forties, we swam in Lake Erie near our cousins' home… when a young neighbor girl was diagnosed with polio, swimming ceased… even in local pools. We cooled off by running through our sprinklers!

Radio news broadcasts and newspapers kept adults abreast of the war's progress, but our days were comfortable and happy. Besides "cooking" on my toy electric stove, playing with my beloved collection of dolls, music was a big part of my life. A baby grand piano was the focal point of our living room. At age six, my sister began piano lessons, and thanks to excellent teaching and learning plus encouragement by our parents, Judy developed her skills. To this day, at age eighty-three, she practices faithfully and performs in public upon occasion. She awes me with her ability. My sister, a first born, has always been highly motivated, no matter what area of her life piques her interest. I admired how she tackled difficult emotional challenges. If she could not manage them alone, she sought professional help. Being the wife of a successful insurance executive and business entrepreneur had its ups and downs. My sense is that Judy's love for her piano became an oasis during difficult times in her marriage. As a testimony to her talent and determination, Judy returned to college during her forties to earn a degree in piano performance. It was a huge commitment for this busy wife and mother of three active young boys. But she did it and did well, but not without exacting a toll. Her family struggled with mom's demanding schedule, and her teenage boys assumed added household tasks like getting dinner on the table. Somehow everyone survived. I, too, loved music. I am told that as a tot, I would take two sticks of daddy's kindling wood, and say, "I wanna play de wiolin!!" My parents responded by providing me with private lessons for many years. To this day, I adore the violin, but lack the same dedicated discipline my sister possesses. Without daily practice, the technique slips away. At least I can still play Christmas Carols on demand!

Playing an instrument (or studying ballet or voice) can teach a child discipline. In order to develop or improve a talent, a child learns to focus, to work hard, and to achieve a measure of success. What a lifetime gift! I believe that when we learn discipline early in life, it helps us navigate our way through myriad challenges. So often in today's world, our children are deprived of that opportunity. But, in the 1940s and 50s, much was expected of young children. We were loved but not pampered. We had our daily chores (no breakfast until all beds were made and bedrooms tidied up). We did as we were told, and we did not question our parents' authority.

Throughout the war years, I was oblivious to the fact that less than two miles away from our house lived the boy who would become my husband. No doubt our mothers shopped at the same grocery store, and we like to think that as little ones, we saw each other at the meat counter and made faces at each other.

Destiny would play its part, and as a freshman in high school, there was a joint field day with my school and John's school. And, lucky me! I was selected to run a three-legged race with John Nevin, a tall, trim, almost skinny, long-legged junior with a light brown crew cut and the most gorgeous blue eyes I ever saw. He must have chuckled audibly over being paired up with a lowly freshman, but he was a gentleman. His smile melted me, and we hopped over the finish line with little effort. I was hooked… although I doubt he had any clue…then.

This three-legged race marked the very first challenge for a couple who has leaped many hurdles, crossed many finish lines together, and who intends to be forever tied together, right to the very last mile.

Adjusting to Retirement

"Don't simply retire from something; have something to retire to."
Harry Emerson Fosdick

If anyone told me seventeen years ago when the company John helped lead was sold that the best years of our lives lay ahead of us, I would have blinked and asked, "Are you sure?" I was not ready to embrace the unexpected change in our lives. We did not have a "plan." I privately wondered whether this might be a gift from above because my husband was a chronic workaholic. I knew that his body would no longer be assaulted by the stress of corporate life. I knew that he had a chance for a healthier life style. But I also knew he would be devastated with the sudden end of his career. And I was right! The first years of John's retirement were difficult, and sparks often flew as we each struggled to find our new normal.

Too bad we had not yet heard the wise words of a dear retired friend who proclaims "retirement isn't a pop quiz. It requires some study and planning." But when a corporation springs the end of a career on someone, there is little time for advance planning. The good news is that anyone who is cognizant can learn to be pro-active long before approaching retirement age.

Ideally, the age to retire is decided by the retiree and his/her spouse. Ideally then a retiree chooses what the "second" career will be. Ideally they plan where they want to live, whether to move to a warmer climate, or to stay in the home where they have raised their children. They contemplate the future, leisurely! They create a WISH LIST of things to do, design a plan for comfortable retirement, and a timetable for it to happen.

These days, however, with a rocky economy, people wake up one morning employed, set off to work, and go to bed unemployed. For corporations, it is all about the "bottom line," whereas in the fifties and sixties, an executive could rely on loyalty *from* his company as he practiced loyalty *to* his company. For example, if a young man began working his way up the corporate ladder in a large corporation, and he exhibited determination and promise, he was promoted. He was not cast aside in order for the company to hire someone "from the outside." Nor did an employee typically "job hop" as is now part of the current career syndrome. Who knows which came first: corporate disregard of employees or visa versa. Over the past several decades, things have changed and employees feel far less secure than they did when John began his career.

Another difference in today's world is many more women are working and have successful careers of their own. Sometimes they are the major breadwinners and their husbands must yield to the demands of their wives' jobs. This was rare, practically non-existent, when John and I were married, and for many years as we were raising our family. When he retired, my life changed, too; but because my "career" consisted of homemaking, taking care of husband and children and volunteerism, I was not salaried. We did not have to cope with his being retired while I was still employed, going to the office and even traveling each week.

These days many couples in their sixties have to decide how they will move forward when one retires while the other one is still working. Obviously this is a hurdle for them, and obviously they need to decide how to make this new situation work best. But equipped with good communication skills, couples find their own answers and their own ways to adjust...an opportunity for more "give and take" as is required of every good marriage.

After my husband graduated from Princeton University in 1957, he immediately went to work for the largest paper company in the USA. John's father was a top salesman. John had "cut his teeth on wood chips" and all things related to making and selling paper. It was a natural fit for him as a graduate engineer to want to follow in his dad's footsteps, although John preferred the manufacturing rather than the sales and marketing side of the business. John was an eager, hard working employee, never a "clock watcher" or worrier about getting paid for the endless hours he spent on the job. After

8

a few months of working in the Ticonderoga, New York mill, John came back to Cleveland to marry me. We were blissfully excited about beginning life together. During the first twenty years of our married life, we moved ten times, including two moves with the United States Air Force. Our first twelve years of marriage produced three children, with a fourth on the way.

Having been enrolled in ROTC during college, John was obliged to interrupt his paper-making career for over three years as he willingly fulfilled his USAF commitment to our country in both California and Kansas. Luckily our baby Allison and I could go with him. We loved living on the base as it felt like an extension of college life. Everyone was young, near or close to our ages. Friends from different states were plentiful, as were babies. Our second little girl Susie was born at Edwards AFB, and the entire hospital bill for delivery and five-day care was $7.50! The opportunity to become friends with neighbors some of whom became astronauts was unique in California. We thrived on the sound of sonic booms, as we knew that test pilots were achieving new records. Occasionally there was a fatality, and we witnessed the outpouring of support and love for the newly widowed wives and their children.

The adventure of military life during the rise of the Berlin Wall era taught us the fragility of peace. To live at Edwards Air Force Base during a period of high alert was maturing. We young wives were told that at any time we might have to evacuate to the underground Boron Mines where we would stay for an unlimited amount of time. Our cars were packed with diapers, water jugs, canned goods plus a few essentials. Our husbands, however, needed to remain on duty. The prospect of a nuclear attack on our base was not an idle concern. Luckily, after several anxious weeks, world leaders simmered down, and the alert was lifted. John and I will always be grateful for the opportunity to appreciate the sacrifices our military men make to protect our freedom. While John never saw battle in Vietnam, as did some of our peers, he did have the honor of serving our country on two vital Air Force bases: Edwards AFB and Shilling AFB in Salina, Kansas. We often wish that mandatory military service still existed so that all young people might realize the blessing of living in a free country. May it never be forgotten or lost.

Because we were raised in the fifties when no (proper) couple in love lived together before marriage, I dropped out of college after my second year. My passion for learning was not as great as my desire to marry John. To this day, I remember my darling father's disappointment that I opted for an MRS degree rather than a B.A. Although my dad loved and admired John, it crushed him that I chose marriage over education, especially when it was given to me on a silver platter. My father earned his way through college and law school with zero financial help from his immigrant Icelandic parents who worked a small farm on Washington Island in Door County, Wisconsin. I will always remember my father's words when he said to us, "Even as young as you both are, I can't prevent you from getting married because John can support you. He has a good education and a good future." My father was right, and so was I to marry John.

As the years passed, my plan to return to college dimmed. I comforted myself by reading voraciously and believing that moving to all areas of the country, even Ottawa, Ontario, provided a unique education in itself. We were moving every few years, we were having babies, whom we adored, and with no family nearby, I had my hands quite full. My husband was wonderful, although often absentee due to job demands. Being driven to succeed, his work ethic trumped his desire to eat dinner every night with his family. To his credit, he never doubted any decision I made regarding the raising of our children.... he supported me completely and often undergirded me via the phone from afar.

Not until we lived in Connecticut and our children were much older did I ever have a paid job. But, wait! From 1966-1968 I wrote a weekly column about social events for our Livermore Falls, Maine newspaper. It was such fun, and I loved the chance to write and earn money. The penurious publisher and owner paid me ten cents an inch. On a good week, I made $2.50! Eventually, my salary was boosted to a whopping nineteen cents! Years later when we moved to Wilton, Connecticut another opportunity presented itself. As a frequent visitor to the local art gallery which featured exceptional artists, I was approached by the owner to work for him. He had a great eye, and he taught me to help customers choose appropriate frames for their pictures, to cut mat board and large sheets of glass, to assemble the required parts into a flawlessly framed finished product. As time passed, I also learned the knack of hanging artwork so that each piece complimented its place on the gallery wall. We hosted successful art exhibits; I became acquainted with talented artists, many of whom lived in Connecticut, New York and much of New England. This opportunity instilled an interest in selling art to offices as well as individuals. With each paycheck, I gradually bought paintings for our own house. After a few years, I started my own business called The Corporate Image. With the booming migration of corporations to Connecticut, there were many empty office walls, and many opportunities to sell art. An exciting opportunity emerged just before Christmas one year, when I was given the opportunity to offer an original Norman Rockwell drawing of a young boy, holding a fishing pole and a bottle of coke to the Coca-Cola headquarters in Greenwich, Connecticut. On a snowy afternoon I drove to the corporate offices, gave an enthusiastic presentation, left the valuable piece with the person in charge of art acquisitions, and crossed my fingers. As each day passed hopes soared. Yet about one week after Christmas the phone rang to come pick up the Rockwell. What a disappointment. The price was unbelievably fair. My guess is that someone at the highest level said, "No thanks." Perhaps the real reason for the loan of the picture was to enhance a wall during the Christmas season with its corporate entertaining. Who knows? But in today's art market, a Norman Rockwell drawing would be valued in six figures.

Between my fun job, church volunteer work, four active growing children, my life had solid structure. Friends became family. Life after sixteen years of living in various mill towns became more multi-dimensional for me, yet I learned life-long valuable lessons from each place we lived. Making lasting friends was one of the best byproducts of a nomadic corporate existence. And at one point, late in John's career and after our children were launched, we owned two homes so that we could commute back and forth between Virginia and North Carolina, allowing us to be together more. Little did we realize, however, as the years flowed from one to another, that when the time came for John to retire, we both would be shocked and ill-prepared.

John was given a few months' notice that his company was to be sold, and his position as a top senior officer would end. Weeks passed quickly as he tied up loose corporate ends. He had little opportunity to think of the future beyond selling our North Carolina condo and finishing his job. On the surface, he appeared in control and serene. But after so many years of marriage, I could see his disappointment. I could feel his sadness that he would never achieve his dream job: to be CEO of a company. I was sad his dream would not come true. Why? I knew that he deserved it, and had earned his dream position; all those moves, all that upheaval we experienced with our four children was geared to achieve John's ultimate goal of running a major company. I had identified with his needs and tried to do whatever was required of me as a corporate wife. A dozen moves proved that. I recall many company dinners I could easily have skipped. I recall tedious superficial chitter chatter. I gave fully of myself as I tried to know and understand some of the more difficult corporate personalities we met. Someone once told me I was one CEO's favorite dinner partner…why? Because I kept asking him questions about himself! That came naturally to me, and it made time pass easily with the pressure off myself. I learned from listening. I realized that most people of authority are comfortable when talking about themselves. I learned what made that person tick. I learned that a person could feel isolated and lonely as a CEO. I learned that although he may relish his position and power, he yearns to be accepted and treated as a normal person. Reaching out to another is rewarding and asking questions about another is a handy tool for easy conversation. As a teenager, my wise mother taught me that secret, and I have been forever grateful.

Being an engineer, John's mind, once it was not filled with corporate matters, turned to the nuts and bolts of our financial future. Luckily, his Scottish heritage made him frugal and fiscally responsible. Good thing for our marriage, as I believe money is for spending! No matter how carefully a couple saves and invests, we soon learned it is scary to live without a paycheck, even when there is a pension and savings plan in place. Few people contemplate retirement before age sixty-five, the optimum time for Medicare and Social Security to kick in.

In my naivety, I did not realize retirement would present another enormous challenge. This came in the form of a major shock to my husband's psyche and ego. Because his "dream job" was within reach, only days away from being announced, we were both dumbstruck that the board of his company chose to sell. It was a sudden decision, with no warning for upper management. I could only imagine how John felt. He had worked tirelessly for three different companies for over forty years. He sacrificed many aspects of family life. Our children did, too. Their father was often absent, and when he was home, often weary. He missed many ball games, recitals and school parents' nights. But, that is how it worked in that era, and John was a dedicated corporate executive. As my mother always told me, "John's job is to bring home the bacon, yours is to cook it." On the surface, we were a "Leave it to Beaver" family. Yet I knew my husband was ill prepared for tedium. His mind was too active to fill his days chasing a golf ball or working crossword puzzles. I worried about having him around so much. He is precious but messy, kind but careless, and he simply doesn't see what I see. I like a clean kitchen, a made bed, and as little clutter as possible, unless I am the culprit who causes it!

Trying to put the best foot forward and believing in the proverbial cup half full mentality, I hoped retirement would be a new marital adventure blessed by freedom from moving, freedom to come and go as we pleased, and freedom to plan our own schedules. I felt cautiously optimistic. For the first time in our marriage, John was no longer obligated to meet his company's needs first and foremost. Our family and I could be his priority for a change.

While it was hard for John to accept that he would no longer be a corporate executive and that his ultimate dream would not come true, he realized it was also hard for me. I hurt for him, but I also hurt for myself as yet another unexpected change was inflicted on me. I had to regroup, to adjust to having him home most all of the time, without a set schedule of how to spend his time. I knew we were tied tightly, but all our married life had revolved around his career and our children. I needed to let go of my long established routine and get over it.

Much to share about this early phase of retirement, but let's leap forward before going backwards. With seventeen years of retirement adjustment behind us, perhaps it is best to proclaim the triumph of having made it through the new struggles and challenges intact. Now in spite of diminishing physical attributes, we can safely say, "we are richly blessed." We did survive those early years of retirement. We learned from our mistakes and from each other. Perhaps that period of adjustment helped us to "bank" strength for the future. Perhaps we acquired more resilience. Through varied experiences we gradually accumulate wisdom. Very few things happen to us that we can't relate to an earlier event in our lives. It is as if we are playing a tune with variations on the theme. Something happens and we say to ourselves, "this reminds me of the time when…" How comforting that can be! It feels as if we have an emotional cushion tucked under us when we fall. We don't hit the floor quite as hard. It may be tricky to pull ourselves up, but we can do it. We have resilience. We can be strong enough to endure what lies ahead. Rocky periods have and will continue to assault us, but we try to offer a prayer of thanksgiving for each good day we share together. These gifts can never be taken for granted, because each day of our lives reveals a new normal.

Learning to Live Together Again, 24/7

The first morning of John's official retirement harkens a vivid mental picture. As we ate breakfast, the phone rang in our kitchen. John popped up to answer it. So used to a ringing phone being for him he forgot that he was no longer in his office. It was gone! All his business possessions were stacked in packing boxes. Life was different. His daily routine was ruptured, and everything felt drastically different. Instead he was catapulted into a new chapter of his life for which he was ill prepared. He looked dazed. I realized he was in limbo. There was nowhere he HAD to be. There was no secretary to present him with his schedule of meetings for the day. There was no need for him to hop into the shower, to shave, and dress in a business suit. There was nothing familiar for him to do, and suddenly his life felt like one long weekend. After forty-two years of corporate life, there was no one to talk to except Martha, our dog, and me. And what must have been even harder for him is that I had a daily life I enjoyed and one that kept my hours without him full and meaningful.

When I say that this was a shocker for John…I should honestly say it was a super shocker for me. I loved my husband dearly, but I was used to my own routine. I had activities of my own, church meetings, volunteer work, and lunches with friends and my own way of doing things around the house. Sitting around drinking coffee all morning was not acceptable. After a few weeks of feeling out of sorts, John, being a quick study, realized that he needed to fill his days with purpose. He decided to launch his own consulting firm. To make that happen he needed "his own space," his own telephone line, and his own computer. Luckily we had a "bonus room" over the garage where an extra TV and our grandchildren's toys were kept. Perfect office space. Soon he had bookcases built, a desk delivered, filing cabinets bought, and John launched AYRSHIRE INC. Progress! A saving grace, to be sure, for both of us. And one sage word of advice from John to all retirees: "be sure to have a minimum of two TVs in your house... and if grandchildren come to visit, don't worry, they will decide what you watch!!"

This period was adjustment with a capital "A". For John, the greatest challenge had to be shifting gears away from Corporate Life, which was the primary focus of his adult life. He was a Type A workaholic. Those tendencies don't fade quickly. For a man as immersed in his corporate career as John, he was "grieving" without either of us attaching a name to it. I understand now, but at the time I did not. Instead, I found myself feeling impatient, hurt and left out whenever he was crabby or in a bad mood. I felt thwarted and frustrated when I could not get through to him. And occasionally, very occasionally, we had some angry exchanges. The good thing is they did not last; the good thing is that we could talk things through while the "storms" subsided. Perhaps our history of loving each other for well over forty years was the reason we could take deep breaths and try harder to listen to each other. After all, a dozen corporate moves did indeed create upheaval in our lives, and working for three different corporations certainly introduced change into John's life. And through it all, the rough times and the happy times, we had managed to build a sturdy foundation for our marriage. And we both have profound faith, believing that God has a plan for us. Trite as it may sound, it is true that the "family that prays together stays together."

One of John's main concerns, and perhaps most significantly, was learning to live without a monthly paycheck. (Later in the book, the Where-With-All versus Have-It-All section will address the topic of managing finances in depth.) He had never, since age twenty-two, been without one. Suddenly, my Scotsman husband, always checkbook cautious (frankly penurious at times), became obsessed with money. "How much did that cost, Joy?" "Have you seen what the stock market did today?" "Have you any idea how much it takes to run this house?" And so forth…money became such an obsession with him that I thought perhaps I ought to apply for a sales clerk job at Macy's to earn spare spending money!

One day when the phone rang it was a life long friend who owned and managed a portfolio management firm in New York City. Miles and John were close friends since college days, and his wife Linda was and is my "soeur du coeur." When I heard Miles' voice, my worries tumbled out as he and I talked, and suddenly he said, "What John is feeling is normal for many men. He is scared…for the first time in his life. There is no more paycheck. There is no NEW money coming in…"

Bingo! I finally got it! Miles' words put everything into perspective. While I could feel comfortable because our retirement portfolio seemed healthy to me, John felt as if the rug was snatched out from under him. He was experiencing real separation anxiety not just from end of his career but from his steady financial remuneration every month. No wonder he was irritable, no wonder he was tense, and no wonder he was questioning almost everything I spent. The sudden end of his career was a devastating jolt. He was catapulted into a new way of life and thinking. Retirement was supposed to happen sometime after he reached the age of sixty-five….not before. As one friend Debbie recently said, "When my husband and I were young, we thought the idea of retirement was absurd." At the time John was retired he was quite young….only sixty-two. He was thriving on corporate challenges, and he was happy because he could see his long awaited "rainbow" position hovering on the horizon. We, indeed, had "work" to do as we learned to live together 24-7.

As John learned how to live away from corporate life, the word spread that he was retired and might have free time to volunteer. With a bit of urging from friends and me, John became involved in church related efforts. He researched and helped to create an improved sound system for our sanctuary. He served as an elder, and he chaired different committees. His life became busier, and as such, more fulfilling. Often, however, he would experience frustration, as he realized that the world of volunteerism operates quite differently than the corporate world. There is no CEO to chart the course, and EVERYONE wants to offer opinions and be heard. Eventually the rewards of volunteerism replaced many of John's frustrations.

While his corporate years provided tools for leading successful businesses, as an unpaid volunteer, his expertise was not always welcome. Occasionally, it was a difficult "pill" to swallow. He was annoyed by lack of efficiency. He was used to action on his terms. He did not like to waste time with tedious meetings. He liked leadership that was solid, knowledgeable, and efficient. He liked to solve problems efficiently. It took some time for him to realize that volunteers are motivated by commitment to a cause rather than to a business model. Volunteers decide their own pace. Happily, however, John became less agitated, and happily he adjusted to the non-corporate world. He has grown, too, in understanding and patience. The depth and breadth of his knowledge continue to awe me. Possessing a quick, retentive mind, reading voraciously also stood him in good stead. Not only could he create a perfect business plan for his volunteer jobs, but he also knew the fine art of finance on a very practical level. For two years he was our church treasurer and cleaned up a messy set of books. Of course, he asked for professional CPA help as needed, but his mind knew how to approach and resolve the tasks. He was a perfect match for the job!

In time he began to make non-corporate friends who were also retired. What a blessing! Especially, since he had never contemplated non-corporate life. He was not a hobbyist, except for crossword puzzles and golf. He did not like to putter in the yard, or tend a garden. I loved it when he joined a glorious new golf club. I loved it when he had a lunch date with another retired friend, or when he met a new golf partner. I was not used to his being "under foot" all day. I didn't want to feel guilty for leading my own daytime life, keeping my own schedule. Some days we felt crowded in our own spacious house. We bumped into each other. A wise friend said that "when older people retire they need to move to a larger house rather than a smaller one." Interesting concept, but not always possible. Perhaps having one's own retreat and designated space is all it takes. John and I overlapped. I did not want him wandering around the kitchen when I was cooking. We had to adjust to sharing our space on a full time basis. Thankfully, John did not "stick his head in the sand." His consulting business helped, too. And, sporadic though it was, for a few years it was a great bridge to full retirement for him. He could feel needed when called to manage a consulting project, and he could utilize his vast corporate expertise. And when we clashed, we kept the dialogue going. We learned to communicate well, without angst. We did not always agree, and it was often difficult for him to grasp my concerns. But as a smart and sensitive fellow, he gradually worked through his end of career grief, listened more carefully, and developed his own philosophy for our new life. I loved it when he said, *"We need to be evolutionary, not revolutionary!"*

For those men or women who choose when they want to hop off their career paths, their transition is less difficult than John's. They plan ahead, they think through how they want to spend their time. Perhaps it is pursuing a long adored hobby or starting a new mini-career. These days there are many options. One fellow we know converted his garage into a fully equipped workshop for building furniture. He spends hours there each week being joyfully productive. He does not miss his corporate career for a second. A cardiac surgeon friend of ours retired in his early sixties. He manages their "farm." It is a full time job of a clearly different nature, and he loves the challenge of raising calves to maturity, getting them to market. When I asked him if he misses medicine, his quick response was, "I miss the patients and my co-workers. I don't miss the new system of health care....." Dick has embraced healthy and happy trade-offs.

Our dear friend Maurice, who earned a Purple Heart in Vietnam as a pilot, came home from his years of service and went to work as an engineer for the Department of Transportation in Richmond. A graduate of Virginia Military Institute, Maurice nurtured strong personal connections as he remained active in his alumni class. When Maurice took early retirement from his government career, he selected his timing. And according to Carol, his devoted wife, he suffered zero side effects as he slid seamlessly into the retirement years. An avid "do-it yourself" kind of guy, Maurice managed his yard, the repairs around his house. He played golf, kept a wide network of friends from VMI, volunteered at the VA hospital and kept close touch with other Purple Heart recipients. Maurice became the leader of a meaningful Sunday school class of older people, and he and Carol reached out with love to everyone in need. Maurice even offered himself up to his friends to play chauffeur to and from the airport so that no one would need the expense of long-term parking! Maurice created a rich, full life, never once looking back to his corporate career with a yearning to return. Maurice and Carol are POSTER CHILD retirees....and I love it that John and Maurice have become great friends and lunch buddies.

These stories illustrate that retirement transition is minimal for both husbands and wives when they choose their own time frame. It seems that living together all the time and blending of their schedules does not phase these folks as much as it did us. I wish I could have made it easier for John. But I admit I fussed when he lingered in bed longer in the morning than I wished he did, when I came home to find the kitchen a mess with his lunch dishes, open peanut butter jar, mayo jar, etc. I wish I had been more patient. I needed to adjust. For years I had been in charge of my own days and my own schedule, just as his career had dictated his dailiness. I had much to learn about living together 24-7. However, I was truly happy to give up our yo-yo life commuting between Virginia and North Carolina. I was delighted to return to our "Happy Ever After 'til the Nursing Home" house in the countryside of Goochland County. I could resume my life. I no longer had to pack and unpack each week or wonder how I could possibly be so negligent as to leave my favorite black shoes at the other house! The effort of living in two places at once cured me of wanting two homes ever again. "We can do a lot of vacation renting, John, for what is required to care for two places at once!" He totally agreed.

The other good news is that those early years of adjustment have become a dim memory, hardly worthy of a blip on the radar screen of marriage. Gradually we both realized a sense of humor does diffuse a tough time. Often laughing is the last thing we feel like doing, but if we take ourselves too seriously, we trip ourselves on our own egos, and we flounder badly. During those early years of John's non-corporate career, I learned the importance of not "sweating the small stuff"...and of old fashioned empathy, TRYING to put myself in his shoes. Raising children and surviving frequent moves helped me to learn the process of "letting go." And over time, my understanding of John's new challenge improved, but not always. We each needed to see the humor in difficult situations, and we each needed to back off and be less intense. The good news is, as we get older, we laugh even more. We hardly ever disintegrate into a bona fide argument, because one or the other of us says something to make us both laugh, or at least giggle a bit.

Choosing Where to Live - Stay Put, Relocate, or Downsize

Many newly retired couples contemplate where to live. Do we remain in the same familiar community, move to a warmer climate, or closer to children and grandchildren? Do we sell the beloved home, downsize to an apartment or condo, or even move to a retirement community? Many decisions to be made, a quandary every retired couple must address. Common sense suggests the best choice is to let the newness of this phase settle in before deciding to relocate to another location or before scurrying out to buy "toys" like a boat or an RV. Thus, a wise idea is to slow down, take a deep breath, and let retirement era permeate mind and body. Proceed at a leisurely fashion.

Soon after John retired, he said to me, "You have followed me all over the country for my career. I know you loved Connecticut and we have two children living in the northeast. It is your turn to choose where we live." As wonderful as it was to be given that option, and as much as we both loved the thought of being closer to family, I knew it made little sense to move back north. The weather with its long winters and short springs as well as the high cost-of-living was the main reason. We had also learned from John's parents who relocated in their sixties to Maine to be close to us that it is unwise for grandparents to become dependent on offspring for their daily happiness. A few years after John's parents left Cleveland for Portland, Maine, John was transferred to New York. Corporate demands and opportunities did not permit us to control where we lived. Remembering how hard our leaving Maine was for John's parents, we chose to stay in Virginia, eventually selling our glorious house in the country to build another one closer to "civilization" with city water, city sewage, and underground power lines. Our four married offspring loved to visit our house but were not happy we were so far removed from medical care. "You never know when you or dad will have an emergency, mom." Good advice, as shortly after that I stood on the porch of our house in the woods, with the Hamilton Beach mixer beater firmly attached to two fingers on my left hand. Making a chocolate mousse for company, I inadvertently stuck my fingers into the whirling mixing bowl to taste the yummy chocolate. Ouch! Neither John nor our neighbor was home, so a call to 911 was in order. It felt like hours before the ambulance arrived, but it did and following a large snip of metal cutting pliers and a few stitches all was well. Our children were right: as we age, it is not smart to live out in the middle of nowhere. We built our second Happy Ever After House nine miles closer to Richmond, and that is where we currently live and will until a few years from now when we move to the retirement home we have selected. Having the master bedroom on the first floor is essential. A proven boon when I broke my foot and when John had hip and knee replacements...no stairs to navigate for a good night's sleep.

How interesting it is to talk to people who are either newly retired or already retired about where they want to spend the rest of their lives. While those who live in colder sections of the United States opt to move south, most native southerners choose to stay where they are. Many of our Richmond friends want to remain in their own homes "as long as possible." Some believe that there is no need to move because they have nearby adult children to take care of them as the years pass and health issues develop. They have infinite faith that if, God forbid, additional help is needed, they will hire home health care. That sounds good, but I know first hand from my mother's experience that option can be difficult, even disastrous. Her story will be told later in the book.

One of the most popular retirement locations for "Yankees" has become the Williamsburg, Virginia areas known as Kingsmill and Governor's Landing. Moving south to Virginia is good for a couple's real estate budget. Houses are less expensive, amenities abound, and money buys more goods and services. Several years after John and I moved from Connecticut to

Virginia, we learned that a new "hot spot" for retirees from the north was indeed Virginia. Developers in Virginia Beach and Williamsburg were building beautiful homes to attract clientele, particularly from the pricey northeast. Early in 2000, a wonderful couple that we knew and admired in Wilton, Connecticut made a conscientious study of where to retire "down south." They wanted an area where they would be nourished culturally and physically. They chose Governor's Landing outside of Williamsburg. They bought a lovely new house situated along a small man-made lake where the ducks swam and birds nested. They were thrilled.

What fun for us to be able to meet Nancy and Doug at least a few times each year for long, lingering catch-up lunches. What fun that they could audit classes at the College of William and Mary and partake of the lectures and theater events. They loved their life in their new home. They made many new friends, and they took wonderful trips abroad and lived contentedly until the devastating day in early 2014 when Nancy was diagnosed with stage four-lung cancer. Never a smoker, always a dynamic energetic person, as well as a healthy cook, a smart and multi-faceted lady, this came as a huge jolt for both her and her beloved husband and only son living in New York City. Suddenly their lives were turned upside down, compounded by the diagnosis a few years earlier that Doug had Parkinson's disease. Being the no-nonsense, practical person Nancy was, she told me, "I am going to live each day the best I can, but I am going to make sure that Doug is cared for when I am gone." With that, she proceeded to purge her house of unneeded possessions, find a competent realtor, and enroll herself and Doug in a lovely local retirement home where his medical needs would always be met. The house sold quickly, no surprise, and our brave friends were able to settle into the new apartment before Nancy died. Her bravery, her ability to deal with reality, her pro-activeness were exceptional. The gift of love she gave her husband and son was unparalleled. She was a rare and beautiful lady and an inspiring friend whom I will always miss.

Although this story may not reflect the experiences of many younger retirees, it is a sober reminder to me that we can never be complacent. We need to plan ahead, to be mindful that the only thing constant in life is change. We need to be prepared to make swift, smart choices, at every phase of our retirement era.

Perhaps one of the best choices of where to live by new retirees was made by our good friends Barb and Jim, who moved ten years ago to Richmond from Oklahoma. Being a hospital administrator since the end of his military career, Jim experienced frequent upheaval with his lovely wife Barb. They raised three children, moved several times, and chose to buy their retirement home in Virginia. All three offspring graduated from University of Richmond and lived in the Washington, D.C. area. Two sons were lawyers, and their daughter married a young man who managed his own company. The signs were favorable that none of the three would move to another state. Thus, Barb and Jim did their research and selected a home in an attractive golf community in Richmond. They were young and energetic enough to start a new life; they were close enough to see their children easily without being in each other's "back pockets." There was space enough for everyone to lead separate lives, with minimal travel time, traffic permitting. Soon after Barb and Jim moved to Richmond, they "church shopped," and found the Presbyterian church which has become not only their spiritual home but the source of many close friends. Being an avid golfer, Jim has connected with great partners and played different courses around the state, while Barb has immersed herself in a meaningful life of volunteer service and caring for three of her grandchildren, who have now located nearby. What an ideal situation for this couple, and how thoughtfully they selected their new city. Now, in their early seventies, they have several years before the time to move to a retirement facility arrives, but they are prepared and planning ahead.

Another younger retired couple we know recently sold their big house and moved to a smaller house in Richmond. They love having their lawn cut and serviced each week. They enjoy the freedom from caring for their pool and flower garden, which they kept in picture-perfect condition. They are happy with their choice. Both their married children live in Seattle, which is fortunate. One trip west nets visits with both young families. Rather than move to "the left coast" which is wickedly expensive and features mostly inclement weather, our friends rent a small apartment a few times each year in order to spend quality time with growing grandbabies and their busy parents. What a wonderful solution! They have created a life of compromise that works for themselves and their family.

Other friends of ours, approximately the same ages, have decided that rather than move to a retirement home, they will resettle in North Carolina, living perhaps in the guest house on their son's property. While appealing, it may attract some risks, in case this couple has health issues requiring constant care. Hopefully this move may be the answer to their needs, just as they envision. As Sandy says, "My mother lived to be 103, so I probably will be around for a long, long time. Bill wants to be sure I am near our boys." Living with or near family as we grow old is the ideal condition for many people, but often it is not a viable option. John and I have four children, scattered around the United States. Choosing which child to be near would be impossible. We love each one equally, but we are lucky to know how to live away from our family. From the day we were married we began a life of moving because of John's career. We did not have the luxury of nearby grandparents or siblings. Now, our married children live in four different states. Making life-altering decisions is part of the retirement process. Our hope is that each choice we make will be a wise one, and one that we will not regret.

Some couples thrive on owning two or even three homes. I admire their willingness to organize and plan (plus the depth of their pocketbook!) Perhaps because of the many, many moves during our marriage, neither of us has wished we had two houses. Too often, we worried about selling one so we could buy another as John was transferred to a new locale. Too often it was difficult to leave family or friends behind because we had to move. Too often it was the mere logistics of juggling repairs and bills and taxes for two houses. We had years of managing two houses during corporate life as we waited for one to sell. As with any move, self-induced of not, there are many hurdles to vault.

For example, the real challenge for many who move to a retirement home is learning to live in a smaller space. This is a challenge that requires not only unloading furniture and all excess possessions, but it also means that you and your mate may feel cramped and on top of each other. You love each other, but perchance you might need to "share" an office, a computer, a TV, etc. You are not used to doing this. However, if one were to have a second home, at the beach or the lake, there exists the option to "run away" and feel normal. People can feel "at home" in their getaway house. They can leave the retirement home where mostly older people like themselves reside and enjoy a society filled with varied age groups. A second home gives people the option to leave their retirement home for a break, it provides a change of scenery…AND, temporarily it is possible to forget being a mall walker or a retired gray haired senior.

At age eighty, my widowed sister sold her five-bedroom house in Milwaukee, moved to a gorgeous retirement facility overlooking Lake Michigan. She has a glorious spacious two-bedroom apartment, including a small balcony, large enough for a few chairs and table. Many of her friends are moving to St. John's or are already living there. It is a comfy compound for her, with a built-in social network of companions: readily available for bridge or book discussion or a glass of wine and dinner.

When Judy has had enough of "THE HOME," as she calls it, she can change locales, fly to Arizona to her condo, or drive to Door County, Wisconsin to spend several weeks each summer in her serene lakeside retreat. She can entertain all her grandchildren, she can ride her bike on the peaceful country roads, and she can live the life that has sustained her for the last sixty years. She is lucky. No wonder she likes to prod and encourage me to get out of our big house and move to a retirement facility. Her situation is not like ours, and we are not in a hurry, although we know that the time will come, as it should, when we must separate from our "stuff," and shrink our expectations and prepare for the last phase of life. Neither John nor I want to be a worry or burden to our children.

As John approaches eighty, I often ponder how much longer we should stay in our wonderful "Second Happy-Ever-After House until the Nursing Home." We sold the first one in the Goochland countryside about 10 years ago, and built this home, closer to town and adjacent to what I euphemistically call John's "Day Care facility" Kinloch Golf Club. While we have far less property to consider and fewer bedrooms, there is just as much "thinking" about taking care of this house. Although we both love it, the time to acknowledge our aging selves and to become practical looms. Have we begun to think about "the final move?" Yes, we are moving forward.

A few months ago we visited The Hermitage at Cedarfield, an appealing and reputable retirement complex only ten minutes from our current home. We filled out the application, toured the facility, and paid a deposit ensuring that our name is "on the list." We feel relieved. We feel as if an elephant is lifted from our shoulders. We told the marketing manager we prefer not to move for a few years, but at least we are taking charge of ourselves the best way we can. We are comforted knowing that once we make the move, we will be afforded optimum care for as long as we live. And if a cottage becomes too large for us, we can move to an apartment. And if we need the assistance of daily health care, that is also available. And if, God forbid, we should run out of money, we will not be evicted. We are happy with our choice of facilities because we want to stay as close to our familiar "neighborhood" as possible.

We do not want to be surrounded by a high security fence in an old section of the city, near a super highway. We want access to familiar stores, to wonderful walking areas, and we want to know people who are also residents. That does not mean that we want to embrace Every Night Dinner at the "Big House," and it doesn't mean we want to participate in the five o'clock cocktail circuit. Rather it means that we want to feel as comfortable as possible in this next and final situation. Are we eager to make the move? No, we are not, but we must be practical. We must transition while we still have the good health to downsize and endure a major move, and we must always, always be thoughtful of our four far away, but loving and wonderful children. Thankfully, we have watched several friends, older than we are now, move. Some have struggled to adjust, but without exception, each couple/person has learned to accentuate the positives rather than the negatives. Nothing is ideal yet making smart decisions eclipses everything else. We must be able to *"release the past into the past and the future into the future."*

It has now been seventeen years since John retired. We are delighted with our present home and happy with our choice of our future home. Our only regret is that all four of our children and their darling families live far away. We can't run over and grab a grandbaby for a sleepover. We can't have a Sunday night supper for the chicks. Our children and grandchildren are frosting on the cake and when we do see each other, we have a great time together. We treasure those visits. But John is "my one a day vitamin." We love being together. Most of the time! There have been rough patches, for sure, but as each year passes, we see the progress we have made. We savor each other more, and we enjoy our time with each other so much. We know each other better. We see the manifold blessings that fill our lives. It used to be that the first person I would want to share some news tidbit with was a close girl friend, but now, for sure, the first person I yearn to tell is my John. We have grown so much closer, perhaps interdependent, in many ways. It is a thrill to realize that our enjoyment of each day has become richer, and the meaning of life infinitely more precious. One could honestly say that we have "put meat on the bones" of our marriage, and it is the healthy, HDL stuff!

A truism of embracing retirement is realizing we must continue to evolve. Some of us take more time than others, and that is understandable. But we must promise each other and ourselves never to be STUCK in old ways, old habits and old mindsets. We must reach out with both hands to touch those who have learned before us, we must keep our eyes and ears open to the stories and examples of others. For it is *not what we gather in this life that matters, it is what we scatter that says the most about the lives that we have led.*"

Coping with Even Older Parents and Returning Chicks

As people live longer these days, many retirees are challenged with caring not only for themselves, but their *really* old parents, plus adult children returning to the nest. Living in a challenging economy as we do, many young people graduating from college or graduate school have difficulty finding jobs. Some may find jobs, but cannot afford to save money let alone live independently. Thus, younger retirees often become a "sandwich" generation.

I remember when we moved to Virginia and John was still working, our last child was a junior in college. For Charley, home was Wilton, Connecticut where he had lived since he was seven years old. Because he knew after graduation he could not afford to survive unemployed in Connecticut, he came to live with John and me. As much as we enjoyed having him, he was happy to visit, but did not like living in the country, not knowing anyone, far away from his friends. He missed college life, and wanted to earn money of his own. Little did he realize how hard it would be to find a job in a city where he knew no one. When nothing materialized quickly, he enrolled in a bartending class. He felt that as he searched for a day job he could at least learn to tend bar and earn some pocket money. Soon Charley was the proud recipient of his "Master of Mixology" degree. He then found an entry-level job with a prominent Richmond company, and decided that as soon as he could squirrel away a few dollars, he would find a place of his own. We loved having him, but although he was over twenty-one, I remember listening for the sound of his car at night. I remember thinking, "I am too old to worry about what time this (no-longer-a) child comes home." Our few months with Charley under our roof felt too short to me, but we all knew it was time for him to be on his own. As he made friends through his new job, he worked with a young woman who introduced him to her dear graduate school friend who eventually became Charley's wife, Stephanie. My mother always said, "God moves in mysterious ways!" A wise woman indeed.

Speaking of my beloved mother evokes another story: one that is painful to remember but etched in my heart and mind forever.

When my mother, widowed for more than thirty years, fell ill and refused to move out of her house, the situation became a nightmare unlike any other in our lives. As plucky and independent as mother was for over 90 years, her decline from good health was swift. Even then, she was determined to stay in her house. It was awful for my sister and me. Judy urged mother to move; mother pushed back. By then it was too late for change, and she didn't care. As an inveterate smoker, mother firmly believed she would "go in a puff of smoke." But it did NOT work that way…instead she developed breathing problems that required oxygen usage; she also developed intestinal problems, and congestive heart failure. She wanted people to come to the house to take care of her. We accommodated her wishes. That turned out to be a disaster. Managing a schedule of un-bonded unprofessional women from afar soon proved ridiculous. Mother insisted upon writing her own checks, but I realized that she was paying more dollars in salaries than there were hours in a week. These women were robbing her blind. Not of her possessions, but of her money. And because these "ladies" were not bonded, we had no legal recourse. When I told mother, she said, "I don't care, I will just pay anyway." Fortunately we were able to convince her to give Judy and me power of attorney, which alerted some of the aides that we might be "on to" them. A few were okay, but they were rare. I will always harbor guilt I did not insist that each person who cared for my mother was a thoroughly vetted, legally licensed, bonded health care professional. Because Judy and I lived out of town, and our mother's slide from health was swift and dramatic, we hurried too fast to find available help. We accepted the word of a hospital associate who recommended the women. If either of us had done due diligence, we might have spared mother unnecessary angst, pain, and financial embezzlement.

When I mention that certain aides "altered" their hours, not all did. But it became very clear that two of the hired women were sneaky and dishonest. Our fault. Sadly, one sly woman attached herself emotionally to my mother. The other was unctuous, and in mother's diminished condition, she lost her perspective. Without Judy or me living in Cleveland, it was impossible to monitor activity at mother's house. And, the worst of the story is that as mother's health deteriorated, one of the women treated her cruelly. Will I ever forget going to Cleveland and learning from a next-door neighbor that she heard my little mommy screaming in pain? Will I ever forget seeing the bruises on her arms? NOT AS LONG AS I LIVE. Therein lies the primary reason I am adamant that this experience will never be repeated in our family. How often I have wished that so many hours and miles didn't separate mother and me. There are many "if only's" about that final stage of her life. Yes, there is regret, too. But I cannot change what happened, I can only learn from it. And hope that no one else who reads this will experience this same heartache. As a result of this ghastly experience, I realized the foolishness of any parent with far-flung adult children staying in his or her own home too long. To be pro-active, in charge of our own destiny while we still have the faculties to do so, is both a necessity and priority.

Some couples face unfortunate twists of fate when they retire. They believe that the golden years will allow them to embrace all aspects of life they were once too busy to enjoy. Occasionally it does not work out that way. They encounter unexpected challenges. It feels important to reveal one such story of dear people we know as a cautionary tale for others. Unless we have a pot of gold buried in our backyard, we must monitor financial help to children, charities, and even friends. Our close friends Pam and Harry spent the first 45 years of their married life moving around the country as he climbed the corporate ladder. As parents of three, they endeavored to ensure their children's comfort and happiness. Prior to Harry's retirement, they bought a large house. Why? Because they wanted ample space to entertain out of town friends and to provide a temporary home should an adult child and family move to the area. Pam and Harry were always available to their adult children, emotionally, physically, and financially. All was well until the youngest offspring asked his newly retired parents to sell their dream house and downsize. The timing was right. By then our friends were contemplating another move to a smaller home. After due consideration, Pam and Harry agreed to build an addition to their young son's house, plus a separate yet connected place of their own. The rationale was that if Grandma and Grandpa were the on-site, on-call baby sitters, this son and his wife would act as loving caretakers as our friends grew older. In return Pam and Harry would baby sit and underwrite all financial improvements and additions to the kids' home. They would serve as the "bank" with zero interest on the loan. When John and I heard the idea, red flags waved frantically in our minds. Delicately we tried to mention our concerns to Pam and Harry, but to no avail.

A few years after our friends sold their dream house and built their cozy add-on home, their son and wife announced they were taking their three young children and moving far away, to western Canada. WHAT? No warning for Pam and Harry. No consideration as to their feelings. Although youth can occasionally be impetuous, thoughtless, and inconsiderate, the worst aspect of this story is that our friends not only uprooted their comfortable lives, but they invested heavily in the new property, paid for their daughter-in-law's graduate degree, gave their son the cash to start a new business, bought horses and built a swimming pool for the grandchildren without considering possible ramifications. They failed to have a legal document binding the young couple to their responsibility. Pam and Harry were blind-sighted, hurt, and devastated.

After their kids packed up, rented a large U-Haul truck and moved nearly four thousand miles away, Harry discovered he was saddled with the entire mortgage. With no legal agreement, he had no recourse to recoup any payments. He and Pam were also liable for tax bills and all utilities. Neither frequent calls nor emails or letters to the son produced action or response. It seems the young couple thought everything given to them had been "a gift" and that they "deserved every penny."

"You have had your time, and now it is OUR turn!" they said. Eventually, our friends were forced to sign the house(s) and acreage over to the bank. Because of this unfortunate "investment," they had to move again. They were crushed. They were thoroughly demoralized and hurt. But to this day they maintain that the actions of their children were not devious. Rather they were spontaneous because an exciting new horizon lured them away, resulting in abandonment of a promise to be there for Pam and Harry as they aged. Pam insists the move was not intended to cause her and Harry pain or disappointment. Naïve, yes, but it reveals a parent's overwhelming love for her child. Realizing their limited options, Pam and Harry rented a modest second floor condo. As devoted friends watched in disbelief, Pam parted with more family treasures. Harry relinquished his tractor and his passion for mowing and puttering in his spacious yard. Although he still does occasional consulting work, he is a 78-year-old prostate cancer patient, recovering from major heart surgery. No way can Harry recoup the savings he so generously "loaned" to his young family. To realize that Harry and Pam's largess was appropriated without guilt by their son boggles my mind and makes my heart ache. It also makes me realize that even if men or women have had successful corporate careers, their PRIMARY responsibility is to ensure their own retirement security. Pam and Harry trusted completely, and they never considered their child capable of such deceit. But it happened, and our friends resolutely take life one day at a time.

Most of us would have engaged a lawyer to draw up a legal document in the event circumstances changed and our kids decided to move to another locale. But we cannot know what feelings or expectations Pam and Harry had. Perhaps they felt that their health and future care was secure, based upon the promise made by their children. Perhaps they felt that they had anticipated every possible scenario. Perhaps they never allowed themselves to consider a radical change in plans by their son and his family. Perhaps they thought that their unequivocal generosity would be an automatic "insurance policy" for their old age. Perhaps they thought that no matter what, they would be "paid back" by their youngsters with unlimited loving care, thus avoiding a move to any retirement facility. Sadly, they were wrong. They were hurt not only financially, but also emotionally. Yet, to our utter amazement and their enormous credit, they have forgiven, moved on, accepted, and adjusted. What a remarkable leap of love and faith. Forgiveness personified. A few hundred years ago, someone wisely wrote these words of caution: *"Be just before you are generous."*

How many of us ever think the time may come when we will be asked to raise our grandchildren on a full time basis? We all love those babies and children, and we love each opportunity to be with them. We savor the times they visit us, spend a week or two, and we are able to know them and love them even more. We look forward to seeing them come, but we are also ready to see them leave! My dear friend Sally has a marvelous expression that resonates with many of us. She calls the feeling of departing grandchildren, "Sweet Lonesome!"

A college roommate of John's who was an usher in our wedding and his multi-talented and wonderful wife created a blended family. Each had prior marriages, but they joined their lives nearly thirty years ago. When they married they had five school age children between them. Their hands were full, but they addressed the situation with optimism and open mindedness. Of course there were challenges. The greatest one for Mimi was her daughter's developing addiction to drugs. As an educator, school principal, Mimi availed herself and her daughter of every possible counselor and treatment. Sadly, all rehabilitation efforts did not last. Each bona fide treatment was sought and tried, costing untold dollars, but the daughter married a fellow addict and became pregnant. As a result, Mimi, at age 70 and Don at age 80 are raising their adorable now nine-year-old granddaughter. The adoption process required leaving their Ohio home for several months to establish temporary residence in Minnesota. The subsequent trials of court appearances, inquiries were incessant. But Mimi and Don's determination prevailed. Their love for each other and darling Eliza overshadowed every difficulty. And best of all, they were granted full custody along with the right to adopt Eliza formally.

Now, three years later, the little girl has become happily adjusted to her new life, and her grandparents have graciously rearranged their lives. As Mimi said to me, "I told Eliza that she may have old 'parents' now, but she will have wonderful opportunities to travel, to see different parts of the world, and to grow up learning many exciting things." Mimi exhibits remarkable flexibility as she navigates her own life through the eyes of a little girl while absorbing the needs of an octogenarian husband. It seems that in today's world, we retirees must be prepared for any eventuality. Mimi is my ideal of one who has learned to change her life to nurture a beloved at risk child who might otherwise be subject to an unhealthy environment, fraught with tension and drugs. Don, with his infinite good humor, is also to be admired as he acquires patience to absorb the constant chaos created by a healthy child.

Another truism of embracing retirement years is being receptive to sudden change. We must always love and support our families as wisely as we are able. If unexpected circumstances change our plans, then we must handle upheaval with dignity and determination. We can never be stuck in how we wish things were rather than how they are. Going with the flow, following the path we are destined to walk enables us to learn and grow and hopefully become the people God intends us to be. Frederick Buechner, a Presbyterian minister and author of several books wrote, *"You can kiss your family and friends good-bye and put miles between you, but at the same time you carry them with you in your heart, your mind, your stomach, because you do not live in a world, but a world lives in you."*

Looking Your Best -
Most of the Time

Many women love clothes and enjoy taking time to focus on what is in their closets and what they choose to buy and wear. Some of us are "clothes horses" by nature. (I think I was born to be one!) Some people believe that as we age, we can get away with wearing almost anything we want, as it does not matter how we look. While understandable, my hope is to delay or even avoid that time. As my once beautifully dressed mother reached her nineties and her health dipped dramatically, she was content to spend her days in her "model coats," which were in truth housecoats. She kept an adequate assortment that she ordered from a catalogue. They were always freshly cleaned and pressed by her weekly housekeeper. Mother loved the comfort of the loose fitting, unbelted style. She purred when I came to visit and brought her one or two new ones. She loved attractive colors and designs, but increasingly she disliked dressing in her traditional street clothes. A trip to the doctor mandated, in her mind, the need to wear slacks and a top. A trip to the beauty shop did not qualify. Anyway, as I watched my mother lose her desire to conform to regular dress code, I felt sad and sorry to see her once sizzling fashion spark fade.

Long ago a Connecticut older friend of mine gave me her opinion of managing her clothes closet. Dee said, "Joy, always make room for new!" What marvelous advice! Another admonition is that for every new piece of clothing you buy, you should give away an equal number. Purging our wardrobe each season of the year, taking unworn items to a consignment shop or donating to a charitable organization is smart recycling. Dee said to me, "If you haven't worn a dress, blouse, a sweater or a jacket and pants in two years, chances are you will never wear it." How often I remember those words. Sometimes I feel guilty as I haul perfectly good clothes and shoes out of my spacious closet, but then I think that perhaps these things will benefit someone else, putting a smile on their faces. That is a good feeling.

Thinking about enhancing this section and how to make it more interesting for more women, I decided to hop onto my computer and Google STYLISH OLDER WOMEN. To my great delight there appeared a whole page of lovely looking older women, dressed in an array of becoming styles. What I noticed most was that each model not only had a different look but each reflected individuality as well as admirable taste. Some women had longer hair, some were gray haired, some were various shades of blonde and some were close cropped. But without fail, each one's outfit suited her perfectly. Colors complimented facial coloring. What does this tell us? It tells us that no matter our age, whether we are fifty-five, sixty-five, seventy-five or more, we can look terrific if we try. We can be ourselves, reflect our ethnic group, our cultural preference, and wear appropriate outfits, while maintaining a look that suits our personality. Some of us like classic styles. Some of us prefer to be a bit more edgy. Some of us like lots of color, and some of us prefer pastels. What I know is that there is no rule of thumb as to how we older women MUST dress. And that is comforting to each of us.

I have also learned over the years of living in different areas of the country that styles vary. For example, both coasts reflect the cutting edge of fashion. New York is fabulous, in that it is the heart of the industry, and designers have excellent opportunities to feature their new work.... either during Fashion Week or by marketing newest clothing to trendsetting Manhattan stores like Lord & Taylor, Bloomingdales, Saks, etc. It is natural that so many New York women are style savvy. My sister has always told me that fashion takes longer to reach the midwestern state of Wisconsin. Even moving from Cleveland to Milwaukee as a bride she noticed the difference. Interesting, but understandable. As for California, I remember living there during our youth when we had zero cash for new clothes. But oh, how I loved the California casual look. No wonder everyone moves at a slower pace, no wonder everyone is more laid back than we seem to be on the East Coast.

Virginia women, like those in the Boston and New England area, reflect a more classic look. I attribute that to the fact that our states were among the original colonies. They were settled by pilgrims seeking religious freedom in the northern colonies and by gentlemen British farmers securing land grants in Virginia in order to raise crops. It would seem that those settlers were conservative in taste and values.

If we allow ourselves to let go of clothes we wore many years ago we do ourselves a great service. Even the fittest of fit women have bodies, which shift with time. We can't help it. Weight simply distributes itself differently, and a great jacket that fit wonderfully well ten or fifteen years ago doesn't look the same now. Maybe our waist is slightly thicker or our arms are heavier. Whatever the case may be, it does make sense to let go, purge your closet periodically and keep up with what looks best on you. Avoid really short skirts, which were great when we were younger. Few women have the knees in their sixties and seventies to attract positive attention. One fashion expert believes the "best skirt length is determined by the slimmest part of your knee...right below, right above or in the middle." Remind ourselves that our clothes need to fit us well: not too tight and certainly not too loose. We can each try to be our own best critic. But if we doubt that, we can ask the opinion of our husband, best friend, or daughter.

Remember, however, that as we age we often develop a "muffin top." That is the sneaky little roll of extra skin that hovers over our waistlines. Exercise helps reduce it, but doesn't always delete it. Perhaps that is because we tend to "settle" as we age. Our height is not as tall as it once was...even by a half inch, so that is my excuse for a "muffin top." Advice from fashion experts is simple: if this happens to you, skip the tightly fitted sweaters, blouses, etc., and select tops made of gentle fabrics that drape rather than cling. Be critical, be flexible and be aware...don't practice delusion just because you happen to be attached to a certain top. My daughters are quite comfortable with telling me exactly what they think about my wardrobe, and that is great! It was my older daughter Allison (who earns her living in retail) who gave me my very first pair of jeans. When I opened the box, I thought, "Oh Lordie, I am way too old for jeans." I must have been in my late sixties at the time. But Allison gently urged me to try them on, and lo and behold they were great! She knew exactly what kind of jeans to buy me. They did not ride down on my hips; they were not cut too slim or fit too tight. Rather they were perfect for this older body. Allison knew and I learned. I felt empowered! Now, I love to slide into a pair of comfy jeans and enjoy a day at home or a walk outdoors.

My great professor friend Linda calls my crisp white blouse with black pants and wide black belt look "the Joy." How much Linda tickles me, and lifts my spirits…nothing tricky or unique about a fresh white over-blouse cinched at the waist with basic black pants. A black belt is safe, but a red or colored belt can be a burst of color that catches the eye. Put yourself together each day with care, and the world will think you are much younger than you are. And, if your feet don't scream at you, get yourself some "kicky" shoes! They don't need to feature stiletto heels, but they need not look as if they were bought after WWII. My mother had her "black moriahs," and as a little girl I detested looking at her feet when she wore them. In those days, she had no choice, but now, fashion designers have blessed us with many options. You can be comfortable and chic at the same time. Because I have had two broken feet over the years, my favorite dress up shoe now is the "kitten heel." It is low but has a great shape to it, and compliments ankles. But, whatever you choose or you prefer, shop carefully, wisely, and sometimes even a bit adventuresomely.

We all have friends whose taste we admire. "Imitation is the sincerest form of flattery" and as long as we don't run out and buy a duplicate outfit, we can learn from friends and be adept at adapting our style to suit our ages and our preferences. My sweet friend and neighbor Betty L. always looks terrific. She is older than I by a mere two weeks, but each time I see her I am automatically attracted by how well she has put herself together. Often she and I stop to chat as she is driving by and I am walking my miles in our neighborhood. It does not matter if Betty is going grocery shopping or to a luncheon, she is perfectly groomed. While I tend to grab a pair of slacks and sweater and dash off to the market, Betty never looks thrown together. I always feel better when I see her. She is a perfect example of being "pretty on the outside as well as the inside." She does not realize it, but she is always a gentle reminder to keep myself up.

Genes do play a part as to how we look as we grow older, as does health. If our ancestors came from Mexico, South America, Spain, Italy or the Mediterranean area of the world, we are lucky recipients of skin that doesn't wrinkle easily. Not so much for those from the colder countries of the world. Thus, everyone is a product of genes. In today's world it is quite common to see lots of blonde haired (older) women, accompanied by sleek and tanned gentlemen on cruise ships and beaches. I have told John that until my hairdresser tells me I am too old for highlights and color, I will keep paying whatever the price, and smiling happily at the reality of feeling, for a few moments, a smidge younger each time I step out of the salon! The last thing I want is for the creeping gray of the root system to invade my entire head. Some women get gorgeous white hair as they age, and they look quite stunning. For women with beautiful bright blue eyes, the contrast with white hair is appealing. My friends Carol, Martha, and Dede are three examples of lucky ladies with those becoming features.

One helpful thought might be that we do ourselves a huge favor by searching for and patronizing the best hair salon we can afford. It is sometimes fun to experiment with hairstyles. Talk to your stylist, ask her or him what he or she thinks is best suited to your facial shape, your coloring, and TRUST her or him to be able to see you with an objective, professional eye. That is their job. They are well trained, and they see us as only an expert can see us. It always tickles me to watch a woman come into the salon carrying a magazine with a hairdo that she wants for herself. I have been guilty of this, too...I remember taking a picture of Dorothy Hamill, the Olympic Gold Medal figure skater, to my hairdresser in the eighties. I could NEVER look like Dorothy Hamill but I wanted to try. Luckily my stylist humored me, and we compromised. But basically, it makes the most sense to TRUST and let your hairdresser make the ultimate decision. And if we don't like the results, hair grows and we can always revert back to our favorite look.

How do we decide what hair color suits us best? We each have our own perception as to how we want to look. When I first noticed a few gray hairs, I tried pulling out each one. What a losing battle! As a pregnant mother in my late twenties, I remember visiting my mother in Ohio who immediately asked me, "Why are you dying your hair dark?" I was not touching my hair except to pluck out the gray. Immediately, my mother marched me off to the drugstore to buy hair color. Not knowing a thing, but liking the shade shown on the box, we came home with "Blonde Jonquil #5." My "partner-in-crime" helped me apply it, and soon transformed me into a young woman that my husband did not even recognize when he flew into town! The rest of the story is history. I have colored my hair for almost fifty years. If I were water-boarded and told to admit my actual color, I would drown. The reason I tend to go lighter rather than darker is that every professional hair colorist of worth has told me that is what suits my Scandinavian skin tone. So, I listen and follow the advice. A few years ago, a new colorist wanted to experiment and decided I ought to "go dark." It did not make me look younger. It was a disaster. The contrast between my hair and skin was palpable. We quickly reverted back to the much lighter two-toned look. No matter what, hairstyles, color, and clothes are all choices that we retirees are at liberty to decide. But taking a chance, asking the advice of others who earn their living as hair or clothing stylists is smart. It is another adventure into letting go, being flexible. You never know when someone viewing your total self through a new lens will recommend a change that you can embrace and enjoy.

Speaking of which, do you want a facelift? I don't, not ever. Call me "Chicken Joy," and you are right. I will always remember the words of my daughter-in-law Joan's attractive mother when I was in my late fifties. (I am about eight months older than she is.) As a believer in and successful recipient of cosmetic surgery, Lynn gazed at me over lunch one day. (Because she is a treasure, and she loves our son, our grandchildren, as well as John and me, she can tell me whatever comes into her mind.) As she scrutinized my face, she said, "You look pretty good, Joy, but you should have your eyes done." I knew she was right, but I also knew I would never do it. Maybe one reason is because I live in a part of the country where few friends of mine have had plastic surgery. Perhaps we are the fossils of the "new age," because many women these days are recipients of surgery and thrilled with the results. More power to them, and I applaud their spirit of adventure...plus their courage.

Talking to a retired plastic surgeon pal of ours, I asked him questions whose answers are essential to share with you. Ron is a Harvard University graduate with vast experience at MD Anderson Cancer Hospital in Texas, Vanderbilt University, University of California, in San Francisco, and Richmond's Medical College of Virginia, now known as VCU Medical

Center. When Ron's wife of 38 years became critically ill with a rare form of Parkinson's, he left his flourishing practice to care for her. Since her death he teaches at UVA Medical College and does consulting work for severe burn patients. Ron is superbly competent as well as a wonderful human being. Over lunch with my husband and Ron, I learned his philosophy about older people having cosmetic surgery:

1. Provided a patient's general health is excellent, cosmetic surgery is okay even into a person's eighties.
2. Regardless of age, health factors are paramount…i.e. anyone with a significant pre-existing condition e.g. taking several heart medications is not a viable candidate.
3. Do not believe everything about cosmetic surgery obtained from the Internet. There are good scientific books and articles on the subject.
4. Meet with a board certified plastic surgeon not once, but at least twice, and if possible three times. Ask every question on your mind.
5. Seek a second opinion.
6. Make an educated, informed decision as to who will perform your surgery.
7. Have surgery performed at or adjacent to, an excellent medical facility.
8. Always remember there are certain risks to any surgery, and the risks increase slightly with age, particularly for abdominal surgery.
9. Examine why you want surgery. A little vanity is a good thing, but do not feel pressured by other's opinions. Do it for yourself, not your spouse or significant other or "to keep up with the Joneses."

For years during my youth, I slathered myself with baby oil and iodine and sat in the mid-day sun. My substitute for surgery has always been buying gooier moisturizer, going for facials whenever possible. But, certainly now, in 2015, cosmetic surgery is safer and more appealing for many. Perhaps I am squeamish, but I can't face the thought of unnecessary surgery and general anesthesia. Rarely it can end in disaster. We have all seen women with one tuck too many or lips that look too artificially enlarged. No one wants that result. Neither should we opt for too much surgery so that our faces become pulled too tight, creating an unnatural stiff look. So, a word to the wise: research the best plastic surgeon in your area, check his credentials thoroughly, and be sure you are electing surgery for all the right reasons: not because a friend or a husband has urged you to do it, but because YOU want to undergo it. Choose the right facility, with, of course, the right doctor, where your care will be optimum. Years ago my good friend Meri Dell went to Virginia Beach where both she and her husband had "work done." It was a carefully planned procedure. Two weeks before the surgery, they were forbidden to eat salty foods or drink alcohol. They followed the regime to a T. As a result, they loved their experience. After the surgery, they were transferred to a lovely hotel type medically equipped facility where they had super care and attention in the early days of their recovery. And when they came home, it was almost impossible to see the effects of surgery. Rather they both looked rested and happy.

Before you opt for plastic surgery, do investigate the many skin treatments and makeup products on the market that can help restore some of your youthful glow. A trip to your favorite department store cosmetic department is worthwhile. Potions are painless, and a good cosmetologist can perform miracles. Once you find a makeup brand that suits your skin and your taste, you will be hooked. You will love the effects, and be glad you found such a simple solution to the Fountain of Youth. The question of whether to wear makeup or go "au naturel" is one that some older women ponder. Hardly any woman over sixty or seventy has such perfect skin that she can look her best without using foundation. Most of us get age spots or broken capillaries. Whether to use only foundation and perhaps a touch of blush is a personal choice. My childhood friend Dede is a perfect example. I am not sure she wears any makeup at all, but she is one of those one-in-a-million 77-year-old women who can get away without it. She is small boned and slender, she wears becoming colors, and she dresses in age appropriate styles. On the other hand, I don't like to emerge from the house without a bit of eye makeup…maybe I have become so dependent on makeup that I don't feel secure. I remember reading about one famous comedienne of an earlier generation. As she was lying in her hospital bed with IV tubes attached to her, she asked the nurse for her makeup. She might have been in her last days of her life, but she was determined to look her best, no matter what. She must have felt the same way I do, and I understand.

Makeup for me makes me FEEL better. The trick is not to be overdone or underdone. When my eyelashes and eyebrows visibly began to thin many years ago, I dashed to the makeup counter at Nordstrom or Saks for help. Wonderful to watch these well-trained young women "paint" an old face, making it look infinitely better. No amount of cream or foundation can wash away wrinkles, but they can appear to fade. And it feels good and makes perfect sense to return for an annual consultation. Our faces change sometimes subtly but always constantly as we age. I wish I could handle Maybelline or some well-known drug store eye products, but they contain allergens that do not react well for me. Itchy eyes are not fun, as we all know. So, I gladly spend the extra money for safer, reliable eye shadow, mascara and eyeliner. Truth is, once again, whether you choose to use makeup or to consult a professional is your choice. Each woman must be true to her comfort zone. Yet, sometimes, it is rewarding to take the plunge into the unknown, ask for super good advice, and see the results. You might be surprised how good it makes you look and feel.

Vanity is not restricted to women. We all know older men who have zero gray hair. Their faces may be seventy-five but their hair is forty-five. How does that happen? Grecian Formula? Hair dye? Who knows and who cares. Is it because they are trying to look as young as their second wives, or is it because they really want to keep themselves up to meet their own standards of handsomeness? It really isn't for us to decide. My sister says she has a friend in his eighties who has tinted his sideburns for eons. She says she has another friend who prides himself on his clothes, never looking un-pressed or faded. He is a dashing man, and it is uplifting to see older men look spiffy. And we can all use a wee dose of admiring a handsome older man!

Shortly after we moved to Richmond, I volunteered at a local hospital. At the time I was in my early fifties, but an image of retired men quickly formed in my mind. It wasn't complimentary. Many of the men who volunteered at the hospital were in their mid to late sixties. I noticed a common characteristic. Of course they were kind, caring, and considerate, ever thoughtful to patients and other volunteers. Many had been executives with busy careers. Retirement, however, appeared to have changed their approach to good grooming. Some had scruffy badly-in-need-of-a-trim hair, others sported ear and nose hairs, and others smelled slightly unwashed! Now that doesn't sound nice, but it is true. So when John retired, and began to adapt a "no, I don't need to shave today" look, I quickly stepped up, spoke out and said, "This will not happen to you!!!" And over time, he has done a good job of staying his gorgeous self. He may spend many hours each day in his workout clothes, but when dinnertime approaches, he will look at me, and say, "oh boy, if I am going to get fed tonight, I better go clean myself up!" He does, and I love it. As I tell him often, "you are one handsome dude. To me you are the best looking man ever!" He likes that, and it is true.

I mentioned John's dressing many days in his workout clothes. That tells you he does all he can to stay fit, even at eighty years of age. He works with a personal trainer twice each week, mostly because he needs to strengthen his core muscles. He also hopes that this will help his deteriorating scoliosis exacerbated by arthritis. When John was younger, knee-deep in corporate life, he loved to run. It helped him process business worries and settle his mind. Years ago my cute Connecticut friend Betty convinced me to join an aerobics class. She did me a huge favor, even though I firmly believed raising four children was exercise enough. But Betty badgered me until I signed up. "We will go to Orem's (the local hangout) afterwards and eat salad and ice-cream!" I remember one older lady named Emily in our class. She was over seventy years old. We all admired her determination, her flexibility and her grace. She had been a professional dancer in her youth. To us in our early forties she was remarkable to be "so old and yet so willing to exercise with us." She was not only a lovely soft-spoken gray haired woman but also a wonderful example of a woman who chose to stay fit all her life. That aerobic class with Emily as a mentor triggered my awareness of the benefits of exercise at any age. Walking is my thing now. And it makes me feel wonderful. It reduces stress; if I am diligent it allows me to eat more, and it is healthy. Truly, these hot days I don't walk enough to merit a chocolate chip cookie, but sometimes I sneak one anyway!

The exercise industry has mushroomed, too. Hard to pass a mall where there isn't a Curves or a workout gym, open up to twenty-four hours a day. I choose to believe those places are for young people, eager to get fit before or after work or before bedtime. They have the stamina for all those terrifying machines I have seen advertised. However, some facilities feature simple treadmills, which are quite do-able for all ages. We have one in our basement, and when weather is wicked, I sometimes make myself use it. Taking a book to read helps to pass the time, and if I could move the machine closer to the TV, I would turn that on and be mesmerized on my walk to nowhere. However, walking outdoors is so much more satisfying. John and I used to ride bikes when we lived in our Crozier, Virginia house as we were quite rural and felt safe on the roads. Now, not only would I be terrified of falling off and breaking one or many bones, but also I don't trust the traffic. It scares the daylights out of me to know that my eighty-three year-old sister insists upon riding her bike early in the morning on the country roads of Door County, Wisconsin, where her summer cottage is located. She doesn't like it when I fuss at her, but she promises she carries her cell phone, to which I say, "But if you fall and crack your head open, what good is a cell phone to you?" She just laughs and goes on doing what makes her happy, and so it is time for me to hush-up and let it go.

Having an accessible pool is a boon to those of us who enjoy swimming. We can swim, walk, bounce, or learn basic water aerobics that will loosen our aging muscles without stressing them. With a YMCA nearby or a public or private pool, if we like to swim, we can get super exercise that way. Years ago there was an engaging movie called *Cocoon* about retirees in Florida who met each day at the pool and shared a class in water aerobics. At the time I thought it was pretty humorous to see all those old people doing jumping jacks in the pool. But I don't giggle anymore. John's trainer told me that swimming, even a few leisurely laps, is one of the best things we older folks can do for our bodies. I count our lucky stars that when we built our house, we also built a pool in our backyard. We thought mostly our grandchildren would use it when they come to visit; but when weather is too hot to walk, the pool is a welcome option to limber tight muscles. Recently, John bought himself some flippers, because a friend told him that if he uses those, he will find that he improves his ability to swim and thus get even more exercise. They fit me, too, but so far, I have yet to try them. Silly me! Never be afraid to try something new as a retiree, unless, of course, it is zip-lining or skydiving.

Aging is a high-class problem. Many people never have the opportunity to live long enough to experience it. They never get to see their children settled, raising their own families to young adulthood. Life is snatched away prematurely, and it is beyond sad. Birthdays are to be celebrated not berated. A hard and fast fact of aging: *"if we don't mind it doesn't matter,"* and if we do all we can to keep ourselves looking and feeling good (exercise is key) we will continue to absorb and radiate the joy of retirement. We may not know how we will feel when we reach the last years of our lives, but we do have the power to handle each day God gives us the best way we can. By focusing on the blessings of being alive and well each day we have, we may last longer than we ever imagine.

Advantages of Retirement with Time to Travel

When one searches the Internet for "retirement" and clicks on "aging," one learns that those older people who spend a good deal of their time traveling are called "Gray Nomads!" "Attitude" plays a critical part in aging. If you keep your mind and body active, you will look, act, and feel younger: concentrate on the positives rather than the negatives, you will BE happier. And if you are lucky enough to travel and be even a part time "Gray Nomad," go for it!

Traveling is a great way for husbands and wives who have spent minimal time together during the hectic years of child raising and career climbing to reconnect. When John retired, we expended enormous effort learning the new reality of being together more. It was not all bad, for sure, but as I have indicated, it took rethinking, effort, and energy by both of us. (It also required a sense of humor on both our parts!) I guess it helps to realize that each of us had to GET OVER IT, or be content to remain in the dust of our former lives. Earlier I mentioned my dear friend Debbie telling me that when her husband was at the height of his corporate career, she and he considered the thought of retirement simply "ABSURD." When you think about it, that makes perfect sense. We imagine being young forever - a youthful delusion. I remember thinking that John would never retire, that we would always be getting a pay check, that we would always be hustling to raise our children. Just as we pretend during our youth that this invincible time of life will last forever, we now realize that if we are lucky the older years do happen even unto us. It is a bit of a shock, but it isn't lethal.

To have the ability and the wherewithal to travel is special. It doesn't have to be First Class on Virgin Airlines, although that sounds awfully appealing. It can be on an AARP bus trip with lots of eager enthusiastic and knowledgeable people. When our son-in-law's father retired, he and his wife took exotic trips to different parts of the world. They did it on a shoestring, seeing and inhaling many beautiful and historic sights. In fact, Conall's father died while walking a beach in Greece. For him that was far better than dying on a golf course or being "shot by a jealous lover!" I don't mean to be disrespectful, but this does underscore a point.

Probably the first real trip John and I had after he retired was in 2001 when we joined dear friends since college and sailed from Nice to Istanbul. What an incredible trip! We gambled (pennies) at Monte Carlo, we drooled at the beauty of St. Mark's Basilica in Venice, we toured Dubrovnik where evidence of the brutal Bosnian War remained, we tromped the ruins of Ephesus, we climbed the Acropolis and we savored many different delectable wines. In addition, we laughed hysterically, we bonded even more closely, and we six said we had never had a better vacation. This was a dream come true. We were all care-free, light hearted and indeed a bit spoiled. We felt we held happiness and peace in the palm of our hands. Shortly after we returned, 9/11 happened, and the world as we all knew it changed forever. Just two years later one of our dear friends on that trip died prematurely of cancer. We will always miss Miles, his acerbic wit, and his boundless joie de vivre. We must have been the loudest most raucous cruise guests in the dining room. Miles was unmercifully funny, poking fun at everyone, every situation, and leaving us with our jaws hurting from laughing. As jolting as his wit could be, his heart knew no limits of affection for his loved ones and friends. A glorious human being with whom to share a friendship…Luckily his precious wife Linda and I remain very close, as with the other special couple on our trip. We all love remembering Miles at his "most Miles-y."

As everyone knows, the ease of travel pre 9/11 has never returned. And each time we get on a plane, there is that wee voice in our heads that murmurs a prayer such an attack will not be repeated. But truly, if we cave in to worry, we surrender to terrorism. And in a world fractured now by mounting terrorist threats we older people may never know real peace again in our lives. Thus, for a retired couple to stay at home out of angst at what could happen is foolish. We have way too much to lose. We must take a risk, we must do all we can while we can. So, Get up and GO! Get Going, enjoy your good years together.

We have learned that traveling with only one's spouse is a special adventure in itself. Going solo with him or her creates an opportunity for couples to reconnect on a much deeper level. No phones ring, no computers beckon. It is beautiful, serenely wonderful, to talk and to share everything with just each other. Funny how you can be on a boat carrying four hundred people and find privacy. It is like getting off the world, into a place where only the two of you exist.

A few years after our memorable Mediterranean cruise John and I flew to Iceland en route to a Scandinavian cruise. What a glorious visit! Being a granddaughter of first generation Icelandic citizens who immigrated to Wisconsin generated a huge spark of interest in the little country for both of us. Thanks to my sister's research and her prior trip, we were equipped with destinations showing us my Icelandic heritage. We saw the little church in Erybakki built by my great grandfather. We saw the charming brightly painted little houses inhabited by the seacoast citizens. We are sure their lives in 2005 had changed little since 1885. We saw the smiling faces of those whose days were spent in the open air, on the high seas, as they eked out a living from the ocean. Everyone was completely unspoiled, friendly and, above all, welcoming. And when they heard that my grandfather Magnus Johnson and my grandmother Josephine were born and raised in the town, a messenger was sent to the town clerk's office to bring copies of documents pertaining to both my grandmother and grandfather. Wow, what a thrill! Suddenly, I felt the Icelandic blood course through my veins.

John and I discovered that seeing the countries of our roots is a very meaningful later-in-life pursuit. His enthusiasm for the trip equaled mine, and we loved what we learned and saw. We had already enjoyed a few trips to Scotland, home of his ancestors. Seeing these countries elevated our appreciation for what our forefathers endured in order to come to the United States. All immigrants are pioneers. Beyond the trauma of leaving their birth country, they must learn new customs, a new language, and a whole different culture...an example to future generations for welcoming and accepting change. Flexibility, for sure!

Imagine my shock looking into faces of the Icelanders and seeing features that my dad and his family shared. Just as Icelanders look more or less alike, with fair hair and broad cheek bones, Scots look distinctly patrician; they have finely chiseled features, bright blue eyes, and handsome profiles. Icelanders by contrast are more rugged looking, but in many ways equally as attractive. So often I would see a man on the street in Reykjavik and whisper to John, "Oh, my gosh, but he looks like my dad."

Cogent advice overheard from one Denver woman: if finances permit, travel to the "more remote countries" while you are still in your sixties or younger. Going on a safari to Africa, taking an ice cutter adventure to the South Pole, or visiting medically challenged countries like Russia are all trips to be taken while health issues are non-issues. That makes great sense. Save the "more gentle" countries like Scandinavia, France, England, Italy for older years. John and I can attest to the comfort also of a smaller cruise ship line where once you are on board, all your needs are met...and you never need to repack at each port. And if you don't want to partake of a tour one day, you are not obliged to do so. Instead you can curl up with a good book and sit in a luxurious deck chair, read, and watch the waves splash soothingly over the bow.

Thus, travel as much as you can afford EARLY on in your retirement. Avail yourself of help from a competent, experienced travel agent, who can steer you to wonderful destinations. He or she may also be able to save you money by anticipating booking deadlines and better hotels at lower rates. When we were in our sixties, we were not as concerned about being away from our comforting medical facilities, our own cozy bed. We were not worried that we would have a stroke, and be shipped home in a box. We carried a vestige of that, "I am still young" philosophy, and we had energy and interest to keep up a wickedly fast pace if needed. Just this last fall, sixteen years after retirement, we took a marvelous trip to revisit European sites of World War II battles. We knew it would be a hectic trip. Totally foolish...we were not smart enough to arrive a few days before the tour so as to adjust to the new time zone. Years ago we could fly all night, rest part of next day, get a good sleep, and be ready to roar. Not so anymore. It takes more than one day to reset our clocks to a different time zone, and the rigors of traveling persist longer. Maybe the fact that airlines are less predictable contributes to the challenge, too.

Another downside to overseas travel in our late seventies is that those nasty airplane germs *like* us. Last fall, when eighty percent of our wonderful group of thirty college friends, now all Sincerely Senior Citizens, caught wicked colds, we realized that no amount of Purell, and no amount of covering your mouth if you cough or sneeze is effective. I believe I chewed Vitamin C and zinc till my stomach yelled, "What is going on here?" Our immune systems are simply less vibrant than they were when we were sixty…. or fifty…or forty….etc. But to cave in to the worry of getting sick or falling or whatever might happen as a deterrent to travel in our later years, is less than healthy. We might not want to head off to Bora Bora or a remote jungle of Brazil, but we can manage the difficulties of airline delays, inconvenient as they are, and we can set a pace of touring that suits our own needs. Plan ahead; be proactive, and GO FOR IT! Many older people do find that as they age, they are attracted to seeing more of our own United States. One plane ride only from many cities gets us to the southwest or the Pacific Northwest. Time changes are not as great as going overseas, and travelers know that if they unexpectedly become ill, they are never far from optimum health care facilities. They are also comforted that in our country, English is the spoken language. Here's to a smart option that can be quite appealing and less stressful on many levels!

To sign up for trip insurance is also a great idea and well recommended. That way, if you have to cancel at the last minute, you are entitled to a refund. Perhaps you won't recoup one hundred percent of your trip expenses, but at least you will have airline, cruise ship, and hotel costs covered. We have had to cancel two overseas trips, and trip insurance certainly assuaged our disappointment and saved many dollars. It is also sensible, if you are traveling to the Caribbean or other more tropical or remote destinations, to consider buying Medevac insurance. That covers your being flown home to a good hospital for reliable treatment if an accident should happen. Friends of ours were delighted that they had it when the wife sustained a badly broken ankle in New Zealand outback country. Although she was treated at a local hospital, it was obvious that her break required extensive surgery. To have surgery in an unknown rustic hospital was not appealing. Thus, Medevac was alerted, a trained nurse and a doctor attended our patient the entire way home, and the story ended happily.

To travel is to prime one's brain and to keep the gray matter charged. How can we grow old gracefully if we don't do all we can to keep our minds alive? There is a woman I know who even after she was diagnosed with terminal metastatic cancer, insisted upon checking travel destinations off her "bucket list." Her husband has been a wonderful supporter of her passion, and in spite of Barb's medical challenges, the couple took some incredible trips, including Central America, China, California, etc. After a heroic battle with her disease, this intrepid lady has left our earth, but her courage, her determination, her faith in God, and her love of life and adventure are an inspiration to all who knew and admired her.

Writing this in the middle of a snowy and very cold winter, I have deduced that we passed up a great opportunity to travel south and escape the frozen tundra. We did not plan ahead, as we deluded ourselves that Virginia winters are usually mild and brief enough to allow us no prolonged discomfort. We pretended this year that spring would arrive early, in time for our long awaited family reunion to celebrate John's eightieth birthday in mid March. Now, with a week to go, I see a fresh dusting of snow, speckled with ice crystals, and I am asking myself how we could be so silly as to stay in the cold weather all of January, all of February, and now part of March. Not good planning! We were not pro-active this year, and have only ourselves to blame. Next year, we will have lived and learned and maybe we will just now be arriving home with freckles popping and suntans peeling after a warm few weeks way.

I have a healthy friend who years ago decided that she was not going to venture across the ocean another time. She is miserable on a rough flight, and accurately announces that "even First Class passengers feel the same turbulence as those in coach!" (At least Champagne can calm jangled nerves and is liberally available before take off in First Class and Business.) She doesn't enjoy or even like flying, but my sense is that my dear pal truly doesn't want to leave the comfort and security of her own home. Is that agoraphobia? I don't know, but at the time, her husband's health was still stable, and as an inveterate amateur photographer he adored to travel, especially to Paris and other parts of France. To watch this couple retreat from an energized and, for many, a very fortunate lifestyle of being able to come and go as they pleased, made John and me sad. The "window of opportunity" later slammed shut, and my friend's husband is a semi-invalid, who even if he could, is physically unable to endure a trans-Atlantic trip. Living in a retirement facility, he has help twelve hours each day. Witnessing this situation is a reminder that we must try not to become Old Before Our Time. I once read an anonymous quote that has stayed with me: *"It is better to light a candle than to curse the darkness."* We must keep on trying, keep our eyes and ears open, and never let ourselves become reclusive. If we do, we shrink our vision of life, we cease to learn about the world around us, and we risk becoming boring to others. God forbid!

Reaching Out and Away from Ourselves

Every one of us, no matter our age, needs someone to emulate, someone whose life is rich to the core of his/her being, and someone who measures their time on earth as an opportunity to give back to others. Our precious friend Bill C. is just such a person. Having fought the Battle of the Bulge in World War II, earning both a Bronze Star and Purple Heart, he is the epitome of what John and I "want to be when we grow up." Bill, now a widower, lives on the coast of Maine in the guest house of his former home which was built at the turn of the last century and was a noted showplace of that era. The ocean view is spectacular; the breezes are cooling in summer and refreshing any time of year. There is a pier where "summer people" docked their boats, and the shoreline is craggy, rocky, and scattered with mussels, algae, and sea glass. A walk on the beach is not for the faint of heart, as the footing is uneven. But good sneakers do the job, and once one has walked a mere half-mile, one feels as if one has had a good workout.

For over five years Bill was the sole caretaker of his beloved wife Lois Jane, a stroke victim. She and Bill were married in 1942 right before he went overseas to fight the war. Their wedding picture is adorable: handsome Bill in his Army dress uniform, and demure Lois Jane in her lovely ivory satin gown. They planned their wedding in mere days, just before Bill shipped out for three years. Their honeymoon was brief, but their love lasted for more than six decades. When Bill returned safely, he and Lois put the war years behind them, embraced civilian life, raised four children, and moved nearly as many times as John and I did…. all because of corporate demands. Bill did well, Lois was a devoted wife, and they were flexible, moving from Oregon to Chicago, with many stops in between.

We met them in the early 1970s at a Mardi Gras Day party in Mobile, Alabama where we were living. Bill's Chicago based company hosted couples from John's company at the festivities, and we clicked. This was a rare business connection for John that grew into a lifelong friendship. We remember when Bill and Lois decided to relocate to the coast of Maine. We remember seeing the pictures of their recently purchased house, and we always said that if they ever sold it, we hoped we could buy it. They were gracious hosts, often inviting us to visit. During our tenure in Connecticut, we were encouraged to use their guest house in June before July 4th when the regular renters arrived. Our two boys were young, and I can still see them scrambling over the rocks, searching for crabs and mussels and anything they thought they could convince their dad to cook.

Because of the difference in our ages, Bill and Lois were mentors to John and me. I loved how she, who had experienced her challenges raising her children mostly alone as Bill traveled and climbed the corporate ladder, would listen to me quietly, offering no comment until I finished. Then, only then, would she say something that clicked for me, and made infinitely good sense. I loved her like an older sister, and Bill had the ear for John as well as for me, as John's corporate demands increased, and my frustration escalated. It was in part that friendship that saw us through the rigors of corporate life, as this couple could identify with us so completely.

The footprint for caring and reaching out to others was firmly implanted on Lois and Bill. Winston Churchill said, *"We make a living by what we get. We make a life by what we give."* That resonates in my heart, and to be the recipients of that kind of giving by Lois and Bill has stayed with John and me all these years. At age ninety-two, Bill has learned to live his life without his beloved bride. Even when the care for her was difficult, demanding, and exhausting, he refused to let anyone else be in charge. He often told us that each night he would pray for patience to maintain the compassion that she so deserved. Surviving several strokes, and being a devout Christian Scientist, Lois did not believe in medical treatment. Thus, caring for her, keeping her comfortable was more challenging than it might be for a medically receptive patient. The one pill Bill convinced her to swallow was a baby aspirin. We visited twice during her last years and watched Bill manage with infinite grace, forever cognizant of preserving his wife's dignity, while maintaining respect for her moods and needs. Throughout it all, Bill kept his cute sense of humor, his interest in the world around him, his eternal optimism that love and faith would sustain both of them. At the same time, he never deluded himself as to the severity of Lois' health problems. Any wonder that this couple, this man in particular, is the inspiration for our own future, whatever it may be?

The fact that Bill and countless other older seniors everywhere, served or serve as gracious and loving caretakers to their beloved spouses, is a growing trend. To be in one's mid-eighties managing the multiple needs of a partner of the same age or older requires strength on so many levels. Paula Span of *The New York Times* calls it "The New Old Age." And she quotes Gail Hunt, president and chief executive of the National Alliance for Caregiving, who says "the aging of the population has thrust more seniors into this role" creating the "Care Giver burden." A survey by the National Alliance and AARP Public Policy Institute discovered there are more than three million older adults beyond the age of seventy-five providing unpaid care to a relative or friend on a daily basis. Duties include bathing, dressing, using a toilet, all of which can be rigorous and taxing as well as exhausting. Bill could have afforded as much help as he needed for Lois, but he elected to hire a sitter to come only occasionally so he could grocery shop or go to church. Bill had, and still has well into his nineties, amazing stamina. Not all older people are as healthy. Thank heavens that some communities offer adult day care, often provided by local churches. This is a valuable mission and relieves many older people whose options for daily help are limited. As folks live longer, the need for adult day care facilities increases. Age may be a gift to healthy people, but it is not to many others...and their loved ones.

Another Poster Child for Older Age is our dear ninety-plus year-old friend Naomi: plucky, sharp, energetic, caring and forever interested in her friends' well being. Each summer Naomi travels to her family's vintage cottage on Lake Winnipesaukee, perched on a small island near the town of Meredith, New Hampshire. To reach the mainland she drives her brother's boat where she buys groceries and hauls her own supplies. In addition, she takes her laptop computer to the island so as to stay in email touch with the outside world. She loves the loons on the lake, the glory of nature surrounding her, and she writes beautifully vivid descriptions of the birds flying into a glowing sunset. When the water warms to a "temperate" state, she swims daily...even into September as the leaves change color. Naomi has promised not to swim alone anymore...but there is little doubt that she couldn't serve as an alert life-guard in any situation. She enjoys her five o'clock cocktail hour on the dock with her friends, too. She is forever valiant, she is fit, and she is a trooper. She makes so many of us smile, and she never complains about aches and pains or getting older. Several years ago she told me something that I jotted down on a scrap of paper. It is something special to share. Naomi said, "If you don't continue to learn, you are either standing still or going backward." How wise and wonderful. She never stands still... recently she wrote and presented a marvelous talk about her war years as a physical therapist, helping President Franklin D. Roosevelt and other polio patients, at Warm Springs, Georgia. Standing erect at the podium for one uninterrupted hour, Naomi mesmerized her audience with her vitality and vivid stories. She is amazing.

The value of knowing and observing people like Bill and Naomi is that if we try, we learn. We realize that if we are lucky we will live long and well. Every one of us needs someone to emulate. Every one of us needs to aspire to being a better person: one whose heart is not content to think only about himself or herself, but one whose life yearns to "do for others as we would have them do unto us." Simple, easy advice that has its roots in the Bible, simple beautiful advice that stirs the heart, and a simple formula for accelerating one's own happiness...right to the end...is that not what our lives are meant to be? May we remember Ben Franklin's wise admonition, *"a man wrapped up in himself makes a very small bundle."*

Reaching out is not only about doing for others, although that is essential. Reaching out is listening, adapting, and working toward becoming more flexible individuals. In my earlier and first book *Get Moving! A Joyful Search to Meet and Accept Life Transitions,* I attempted to present moving as a metaphor for accepting change in life. The longer I live and the more adjustments we make to a new phase of life, the more convinced I am that fourteen moves (the last two were local) helped make retirement an easier passage. After his corporate career ended, when John was struggling, I could often step back, assess the situation and realize what was happening. It did not necessarily make it easier, but it helped illuminate the situation. It helped me gain perspective. We women, according to many friends of mine, are by nature more flexible. I agree. We are the ones whose job is to raise the children, to manage the house, and to roll with the punches.

Thus, for those of us who honored specific roles in life, who may have spent thirty-five to forty years living in one house, having the same predictable routine, retirement and the changes it involves are daunting. For one thing, when one decides to downsize, even to a smaller house or to a retirement home, the idea of purging forty years of stuff from one's house makes us want to hide under the covers. The beauty of having moved frequently is that whenever we moved, we HAD to clean out our houses. To this day, I think about marching all my girls' Barbie dolls out the front door of our Maine house, telling the children to pick out the toys they had outgrown and we would give them away. Have they ever really forgiven me? Maybe not, but I hope so. If nothing else, it may have helped our children learn to let go, go forward, and accept change as it happens. That is what flexibility means.

So, as we contemplate the act of reaching out in older age, we also understand the importance of keeping our minds alert and our eyes open. We accept that we never have all the answers, although in the back of my mind, I believe that maybe, just maybe one minute before we die, we will realize, "I get it, I really get the true meaning of life." Hopefully that will be a blessing bestowed upon each of us.

Another meaningful and enduring advantage of retirement is finding projects to involve us that benefit others, and enrich our appreciation for other people's challenges. As a mostly stay-at-home mom without a designated professional career, I spent years as a volunteer in our children's schools, our churches, hospitals, or community efforts. It has been a great source of learning and comfort. When we moved to Richmond from Connecticut and I felt quite adrift, I realized that the antidote for my loneliness was in doing something for others. Volunteering at the hospital, taking a hospice training program, and visiting those in the last stages of their lives became a richly rewarding experience. At first I was terrified that I would not find the right words to say to hospice patients. But that did not happen. Some patients wanted to talk, tell their stories, while others did not. One darling gentleman wanted me to read him articles from the *Wall Street Journal* and discuss them. He also told me that his favorite pie was lemon meringue. I will always remember how his eyes sparkled with delight at the sight of my freshly baked pie. He ate a large piece, fell asleep with a smile on his face. Another gentleman told me he wanted to see Disney's *Pinocchio* before he died. I bought it and we watched it together. Shortly afterwards, the dear fellow died peacefully and painlessly. Experiencing the courage of terminal people taught me more than I can say. I felt better as I was no longer wallowing in myself. The act of doing for others can never be underestimated. Without our even realizing it, we gain strength, momentum, and understanding. I also felt better able to nurture my own mama as she entered her final stage of life.

As with all aspects of life, even volunteer time evolves. The question to ask oneself is "when is it time to step down and let younger people do the job?" In this context I think about all the years of serving on church committees, of chairing events, and of being a four time Ruling Elder, which in the Presbyterian Church involves a three-year commitment for each class. When do we acknowledge that we have served to the extent of our usefulness? Maybe when we look around the "conference table" and realize we are older than everyone by several years. Maybe it is when we fidget during meetings that last beyond 9 p.m. Maybe it is when we twitch with a tinge of impatience over seemingly innocuous tasks at hand. Maybe then it is time to realize God is calling us to do something else, to learn something more, to give something new. There is always an opportunity to give of ourselves, no matter our age.

I read an article written for the *Atlantic Monthly* by a fifty-seven year old man who proclaimed proudly that he wants *"to die at the age of seventy-five."* In his opinion living longer is a waste of everyone's time, patience and energy! I blinked as I read his words, because I thought he was teasing. But, no, the writer was quite serious. Although he admits, *"death is a loss,"* so is *"living too long. It renders many of us, if not disabled, then faltering and declining, a state that may not be worse than death but is nonetheless deprived. It robs us of our creativity and ability to contribute to work, society, the world. It transforms how people experience us, relate to us, and most importantly how they remember us. We are no longer remembered as vibrant and engaged, but as feeble, ineffectual and even pathetic."* The article continues to berate age, and I forced myself to finish reading it. In eighteen more years if I am still alive, I will be ninety-five. And I will "bet the farm" that before this man turns seventy-five, he will "whistle a different tune." To be fifty-seven years old and incredibly naïve is unbelievable. His writing, while well crafted, reveals a lack of wisdom, maturity, as well as a low opinion and regard of older people. Good news is that everyone in life has the capacity to change, to embrace new ideas and to move forward. Why did *Atlantic* publish this article? Probably because the editors knew it would invite many letters, and probably because they are paying homage to public outcry for sensationalism in journalism. Who knows, but part of me would love to write an article extolling the blessings of life after seventy-five.

In *Get Moving* I wrote that a church is always welcoming to new people in a community. Moving to Virginia presented opportunities to join not one but two wonderful churches, not concurrently, but consecutively. As the daughter of a Presbyterian father who served his beloved church in all capacities, I was taught that the highest honor bestowed on a member of the congregation was the office of Elder. I was taught that you need to earn that honor, and because of wanting to emulate my father, I aspired to do the same. And thus, serving as a Ruling Elder not once, twice, but four times has filled my life with many meaningful experiences and opportunities. There is no question it has been an energizing growth period. Now, as my late seventies arrive, I realize it is time to move aside. It is time to "make room for new." How do I know this is true? Because occasionally I feel myself railing against new ideas and goals. The last thing on this earth I want to be is a KNOW-IT-ALL, or someone who is unyielding and stubborn. I don't want to outstay my usefulness. I don't want to be the "oh here comes that old lady" Elder. I don't want to be boring and tedious. This can happen unwittingly as years tick by. We get caught up in our responsibilities, and we feel certain we can figure out most problems. Young people are not expected to understand us older folks. Although we remember how we felt when we were young, they have no clue how we feel or think. They should not be expected to know. By virtue of youth and inexperience, they are too far removed. They haven't walked in our shoes. But we have walked in theirs, even though society now accommodates different trends, actions, and attitudes.

Thus, whether it is church, women's clubs, or board positions, there is a logical time to fade into the sunset. An older person can continue to contribute, but in different ways. If we possess a particular talent, we can share it. For example, my sister is an excellent pianist, and she derives great joy playing for her fellow residents, or "inmates," as she loves to say. This works to her advantage and to other people's enjoyment: it is a perfect opportunity to keep her fingers nimble and to enable others to enjoy her gifts. Naomi lets her friends know "I care about you and am thinking about you." We can volunteer for a quick project, such as delivering flowers to the sick, or baking cookies for a special reception. Truth is, we can give of ourselves, being good stewards of the blessings we have received. We can reach out, touch and love others with all of our hearts, souls and minds. Indeed we can "*do what we can with what we have, where we are in our lives.*" And another thought is: "*We can make a living by what we get, but we can make a life by what we give.*"

Where-With-All Versus Have-It-All

How fortunate some retirees are to have a carefree financial life, providing freedom to come and go as they please. Would imagine that the percentage of those retirees ranks far lower than the number of those who must watch what they spend. As I mentioned earlier, it was a huge jolt for John to discover that the "paycheck" days were over...rather we had to assess our assets, compute the retirement benefits and cash flow, and adjust accordingly. No one wants to touch capital until the time comes when it is absolutely necessary. God forbid we outlive our money!

Like most couples, we have learned, we have made the transition, and been grateful when the stock market is bullish and on an upward trajectory. But in 2008 our country suffered a severe recession. The market plunged. Not only did young men and women lose jobs, but also many seniors on fixed incomes lost chunks of their investment income. Scary! The economy slowed dramatically and disposable income froze. For retirees to put their savings into the hands of a competent financial manager is a very wise move. And the advice we have always heard is that we should never "put all our eggs in one basket." Different portfolio managers have different styles of investing, and at times one might be more productive than another. Some folks like to manage their own money and they do well. However, that can be risky. Unless one is properly educated and trained in the world of finance, he or she is not apt to know how to navigate the ebb and flow of the market, when to buy or sell bonds. We are lucky to have our son Sam, who has his own firm, and who is a wonderful shepherd of our portfolio. I tell him we are his best customers, because our loyalty factor is off the charts! He is smart, has had well over twenty years of experience in the business, earned his MBA with honors at NYU Stern School of Business, so his credentials are solid.

The reason I include this information is not to toot Sam's horn, but rather to alert everyone to the importance of finding a professional financial manager with excellent training, experience, and a successful track record. Years and years ago, we trusted a young CPA to do our taxes. John and I met him, thought he was "nice and knowledgeable." We also liked his reasonable fees. (Remember the traits of a Scotsman.) Uh oh, little did we realize his youthful inexperience would result in incompetence. When the IRS sent us a penalty bill for unpaid taxes, we understood our mistake *and his*. Of course we survived, we learned, and moved on to a firm with an excellent, proven reputation. To this day we still use this New York City firm with great satisfaction.

Thus, besides a competent accountant we need a money manager whose character and record are flawless. During my mother's later years, she engaged a fellow from a major national brokerage firm to handle her money. She had enough to keep her going for the rest of her life with a bit left over. Granted my Depression survivor widowed mom could be rigid, and she refused to let her advisor invest her money aggressively. My sense is that a more competent money manager could have helped educate her more wisely. My mother was physically old, yet mentally sharp. Thanks to our son Sam, he did advise her to be pro-active in her estate planning. Of course, she adored him, but he knew his business, too, and he was able to make perfect sense to her. That is the kind of advice her own broker should have dispensed rather than just buying and selling stocks, which is tantamount to churning an account. Legal but more self-serving than ethical.

A helpful article about newly widowed women was printed in the September 4, 2015 *New York Times*. It pertains to the need for every woman to be cognizant of her family's financial situation. She needs to understand it in the event something happens to her spouse. This is worth mentioning because like so many other women in this country, I have abdicated the management of our funds to my husband. When he worked for large corporations, I balanced my own checkbook, kept track of my spending.

He oversaw everything else: our investments, our mortgage payments, big bills and taxes. I paid little attention. When he retired, I virtually turned over my checkbook for him to balance each month, as numbers and I are not best friends. So, reading this article about a young fifty-eight year-old woman, whose husband died unexpectedly, was a wake up call.

Although this woman was employed herself, she found that she was vulnerable financially. She also learned that although her husband intended to take out more life insurance, he never completed the paper work before he died. Money from an additional policy would have "helped to ease the burden of medical bills that trickled in after his death." This poor woman was caught unawares because she was ill informed. Diminished income is also more significant when a younger aged husband dies first. Typically "household income for women declines thirty-seven percent after a spouse dies." Now this figure pertains to people who are not retired, obviously, but the article supports the belief that "many people do not plan for income needs after the first death in a couple. And retirement planning is more of a struggle because life expectancy is longer," says David Littell, program director of the American College of Financial services, which offers financial education for securities, banking and insurance professionals.

Also included in this article was some sage advice for women: to "know where things are, such as life insurance policies, safe deposit boxes and keys, investment accounts, etc." Women are advised to have their own accounts, "an extra stash of money that's not just for emergencies and their own credit cards." When one older husband learned this advice, he turned over the checkbooks, the main monthly bills to his wife. She learned "how to budget and about their investments. I didn't want to do it. I thought it was boring, but he thought he would go first, and I needed to prepare. He was right." This lady's husband did die first, but by then she was well prepared to handle the financial responsibilities imposed upon her. This is excellent advice for each of us, and as the article also said, "women are receiving more attention from banks and other financial institutions...more and more women control wealth, so they have to know their sources of income." After reading the entire article one becomes alert to the important need for all women to be able to function financially on their own. I admit I am way behind, have much to assume and absorb; and time to wake up is now. We are never too old to learn...I hope.

Money is a touchy subject for many people, but even more so for those whose livelihood is dependent upon their savings, their pensions, and their social security. One couple we know and like decided during the 1990s, the heyday of the real estate bubble, to invest their entire savings in two large North Carolina beach houses. When they bought the houses, the real estate market was flourishing, with no ceiling in sight. They poured their money, hearts, and souls into furnishing and maintaining the houses. For several years they were able to rent them to capacity. Then came the Recession of 2008. No need to tell you that for many people "disposable income" dried up. Vacations were cancelled, and the rental market was flat. For our friends, and others in the same boat, this was deplorable. They were stuck with two houses, both of which absorbed their savings. If they wanted to, they could not sell at that time. Although I don't know the vitality of Outer Banks beach real estate, it is possible it may never achieve its previous high. The U.S. economy, we are told, has recovered fairly well, but there are still many jobless people.

Realizing the hazards of owning two vacation homes and being in their late seventies, our friends have reluctantly decided to put one house on the market. So far, there are no nibbles, but all reports say our economy is improving. Many of us skeptics are not sure, as we must deal with the negative changes in health care costs, increased taxes, and a world situation that is tenuous at best. Hopefully, all will work out for this dear couple, the house will sell, they will earn a profit, and they will find a competent person to invest their earned money. This is a perfect example of putting "all eggs in one basket"...real estate. It looks good on paper to own hundreds of thousands of dollars in property values. But if land or houses cannot be sold, they become a money pit.

Before John's brother died of pancreatic cancer, he felt he had created a solid financial package for his wife, Tommi. Truth is, Jim was too heavily weighted in land ownership. He died prior to 2008, before the crash and luckily his wife sold their big house in the small town of Danville, Virginia. Being a successful surgeon, Jim was an idealist in many ways. His business expertise was limited, although his medical knowledge was infinite. For years John tried to help him grasp the idea of having a more balanced portfolio, but Jim loved owning property. He was sure that if necessary, it all could be quickly converted into available cash. Not so.

Ever since his death, his widow has struggled to make ends meet. Jim would cringe if he knew how hard it was for her to sell a vacation house and property or to unload remote acreage in the hills of North Carolina. I will always remember Jim's taking us to see that mountainous land. It was wooded, steep and I was sure bears were hiding behind every tree. To assuage my fear, my brother-in-law told me he was bringing his gun. I had my trusty "bear whistle," and off we went. Of course, we never saw a bear, but I nearly wore myself out tooting that whistle! Everyone laughed, except me, and at the end of the trek, Jim said, "Okay, Joy, now I will teach you to shoot a gun." He did and it was a new, exciting experience...never to be repeated.

We learn as we watch how others handle tricky situations. One of the most frustrating things anyone can do is to panic during a stock market slump and sell every share of stock. But people do that, and as my son says, "it is as if they are saying the world is coming to an end: that all free trade and commerce will end." Smart message to remember, and hopefully, this should be a deterrent to anyone with fleeting or far out ideas. Of course, money matters are sensitive and so personal that we feel defensive. We are wise to keep our eyes open, to observe which money management techniques are most effective. We are wise to choose a portfolio management firm carefully. Research every aspect of it, check references, talk to clients you may know who use it.

Having a designated person in charge of your assets is a key lesson. It really doesn't matter the size of your portfolio. There are competent experts who will take smaller investments in addition to the large ones. When you shop for a manager, be sure to interview the person who has direct responsibility for your portfolio. It is vital to know what arrangements are in place if something should happen to your "caretaker." You need to know who will replace him or her. Your manager must be respectful, personable, and available to answer your questions whenever they arise. Some people turn over their assets to a large bank trust department. Perhaps it works well for them, but to me it feels quite impersonal. A divorced friend of mine did that, and occasionally I hear her express frustration. She does not seek change, so my sense is she will keep everything status quo. Life is too short to be stuck, but life experience does make us who we are. If we can only *"release the past into the past and release the future into the future,"* we might be able to achieve a happier now. Our "Have it all" could be so much better!

Pushing Versus Pulling: Are We Receptive to Change?

A Frenchman named Nicolas Boileau-Despreaux once said, *"Every age has its pleasures, its style of wit, and its own ways."* But every age has its challenges, and as we age, those are what attract our attention most, or should. Rigidity, at best, is an unpleasant condition. It can be acquired or it can be inherent, but mostly I think it is inbred in many of us. What it means is that those of us who are unyielding may never have had any reason to change. Maybe we have never had to uproot our lifestyles against our wills. We have had things fall into place as we have planned. Few of us are so blessed or cursed as the case may be. After a stable and easy childhood, living in one house for my first nineteen secure years, marriage and frequent moving taught me a great deal. Moving twelve times with a workaholic husband in twenty years from one area of the country to another as our family grew to four children, taught me that with help when necessary I can survive. I can adjust, and like it or not, I have learned to be flexible. (But in all honesty, not about manners or politics!) Hopefully this is a lesson I will carry with me all the rest of my life. Time will tell. Retirement Home years lie ahead. We will unload beloved furniture; blow goodbye kisses to our screened in porch, our pool, our patio, our lilac bushes and dogwood trees. We think, and we hope and pray, we can do this well, without being PUSHED or PULLED by our children into making this decision. We want to do it on our own, and at the most propitious time before we get creaky and cranky. We are already watching good friends come to their senses and make the move, and most are doing it on their own, and are serving as great role models to us.

Rigidity, as we know, means "not flexible or pliant." It is a term sometimes used to describe someone with a muscular disease. My father's Parkinson disease turned his body into an unforgiving, stiff, skeletal frame. But, for many years it did not alter his determination to try to conquer his frailty. How painful it was to watch him try to get out of a chair, to stand up unaided. As the disease progressed it was heartbreaking to know he could not even roll over in bed by himself. But physical infirmity slams us when we least expect it. That can't be helped. But what about emotional rigidity that identifies a person who refuses to accept new ideas or concepts? Is that not unfortunate? We all have a touch of it. The trick is to recognize this trait and to address it. That can happen once we become aware and alert. We must consciously give ourselves permission to change, to become willing to embrace new ways of thinking and doing things. We must be determined not to be stubborn and stuck in a rut.

Perhaps the most difficult aspect of aging for me so far is recognizing the reluctance/refusal of others in our circle to be either PUSHED OR PULLED. Some of these people are casual acquaintances, but others are near and dear to us. Truth is, I have a very difficult time accepting another person's rigidity of thinking or action when I feel they are on the "wrong track." I struggle with those who believe they have all the answers; those who refuse to embrace new ideas or enlightened thinking. In reality this is my problem far more than it is theirs. Years ago when I was a hospice volunteer, I remember an elderly patient who was dying of cancer. She was living with her daughter, and their relationship, which one would hope would be loving and respectful, was fractious and volatile. Each time I sat with this terminally sick lady and heard her complain about her daughter, her primary care taker, I tried to point out her daughter's assets. This woman would have none of it, and when her daughter was in the house, it was obvious that neither one was willing to change the unhappy dynamic. Sadly, it was also apparent that underneath all the stress and angst, they loved each other. What had gone wrong? Why were they wasting the little time left by being angry at each other? Why hadn't this cancer brought them closer together? I felt powerless, frustrated, and miserable each time I left that home. In telling my hospice "boss" about the situation, she said, "Joy, your job is to listen; you can't change anything." I struggled with that statement, but my supervisor was correct. Since then I have found that no matter how hard I try to influence the thinking or attitude of someone I love, I am unsuccessful. I can neither push nor pull someone to embrace a new attitude or way of doing things. This is difficult, but critical to remember those wise words told me many years ago…"Listen. Don't try to change."

Later in this book we will talk about Duct Tape and how important it is for parents of adult children to have a roll at the ready all the time. I get it, I need it, and I use it, but not as frequently as I should. Of course, having been raised by parents who always tried to see the goodness in people and in life, I appreciate how much each person has the right and the need to figure things out for themselves. But isn't it sad that sometimes when age hits us like a lightning bolt and there is way more sand in the bottom of the hour glass than in the top of it, we see answers to questions that are not ours to answer? Isn't it too bad that we can't reach out and spare those we love the heartache of choosing a rocky hill to climb rather than a smoother paved road? Isn't it always a parent's yearning to rescue rather than watch helplessly with duct tape plastered over our mouths? My mother's "pot on the stove" (you will read more about that later in the book) was a marvelous trick for making John and me grow up. It was what we needed…but I also remember asking questions of my mother, late in her life, and by then she allowed herself to tell me what she really thought. That was not often, but she did, and when she did, I listened…. maybe I yearned to know her innermost thoughts so as to accelerate my own learning process. Maybe her timing was perfect. She stayed quiet until I asked, and then, she offered up her opinions.

Perhaps the worst time of life for becoming rigid as a poker stick is later life. Retirement allows us to make the most of our own choices; it allows us to arrange our own schedules, and to plan our daily activities as we wish. But it is easy to become self-centered. That is why it is so important to reach out and do for others, as we have already determined. The thought of moving from our comfortable long time beloved homes causes hard core resistance for many of us. Parting with treasures, acquired or inherited, affects us. At this moment a dear long time friend of mine is mired in her imminent move to a lovely retirement facility. She knows it is time because she has severe arthritis and lives alone in a two-story house, but she simply does not want to make the move. Her family is "pushing" her because her married children worry that if she were to fall, how would they care for her? They are knee deep in their own lives, their active children, and their own careers. They can't be full time caregivers to their aging mama. Luckily their mom is in a financial position to afford one of the nicest facilities in the state. Intellectually, she understands the need, but emotionally she finds it shattering. Her feelings are normal and understandable to me. But now she must dispute her offspring as they try to PUSH her to make difficult decisions about her possessions. This is terribly hard on everyone. My (unsolicited) solution is to offer the offspring one chance to review the items that won't make the move. Choose what they want…then hush. Next, hire a professional to dispose of the unwanted "stuff." That could remove angst and simplify the process. My sister taught me so much when she brought her three sons to select which family pieces they wanted. They did, and she shipped their choices. Then, she purchased a large packing box for each grandchild, and deposited "treasures" into each container carefully marked for that child. She again paid for the shipping, and voila, she was finished with it all!

I do ache for my friend, however. What a struggle to go "gracefully," to the new apartment. "It is too small, Joy; there is no room to put anything." Truth is there are two bedrooms, a generous living room, and a small kitchenette. Meals are provided, so cooking space is hardly a necessity. But the crux of the problem is my friend's difficulty to "let go." I tell her that she has proven she is able to do it…after all, she was the primary family member responsible for dismantling her parents' two homes, and she made good decisions when she left Ohio for Virginia. So I assure her she has achieved success. But we all know that this move to the retirement home is our final move: the one before heaven. It is a momentous time of life, and as pragmatic as we try to be, it is heart wrenching…. Life does not continue as we wish it could be. None of us is exempt. The clock keeps ticking.

Many nights before going to sleep, I think about when John and I must leave our second and last Happy Ever After House. We adore this house… we designed and built it, and it has provided numerous happy times for us, our far-flung family, nearby and far away friends. This year we celebrate ten happy years of living here, and that is a beautiful blessing. We have the space to entertain many friends and family. BUT, we cannot deny the effort it takes to maintain our home. John's mobility is diminishing, due to his scoliosis, and my stiff old joints don't want to scrub and wash and clean as they once did quite willingly. We have to hire someone now to ready the porch for summer, to power wash it, to bring up all the outdoor furniture from the basement. We used to do it all ourselves, but not any more. It would not be smart and our bodies aren't strong enough. Truth is, we must decide without being pushed or pulled. We need to know the right time to put our house on the market and go to Cedarfield. I don't want our children wringing their hands, saying, "Oh boy, we gotta get mom and dad out of their house before they end up falling apart on us."

The PUSHING versus PULLING phase of life is a reality. Some of us may never have to face it, but probably most of us do. Maybe we can afford a full staff of people to come live in our home and care for us until we die. But for most of us on this planet that is a pipe dream. If we can live each day and adapt one healthy mantra, it is "Let go, let God." I pray that we keep in daily touch with God who sends us signs and warns us when we need to listen. As I walk with awe all over our beautiful Kinloch area, I look for indications that we are reaching the end of our time here. I want to wake up one morning, and say, "Okay, God, let me tell John it is time for us to leave this beautiful home. I am ready to go forward and do what we both know must be done. I am ready to spend the rest of my days with you wherever we need to be, not necessarily where we want to be. But where we should be...you and I will go without being PUSHED OR PULLED."

Challenging Health Crises: Unexpected Claps of Thunder

The sudden onset of a medical crisis can feel like a slap in the face or a sudden clap of thunder. It hits hard; it is terrifying. It jolts us out of complacency. Youth for most of us is a healthy time, a "cold in the nose" time of life; middle age is an era of physical and bodily changes with male and female menopause, hot flashes; yet older age makes us susceptible to more significant events. Even though our life expectancy increases exponentially with each generation, our bodies naturally age. Simple viruses can morph into bacterial infections, requiring antibiotics. A common "bug" bites harder, even though most of us try as hard as we can to "beat back the clock," by staying fit, eating well (mostly), avoiding junk food (mostly), and exercising regularly.

Hardly a week passes now that someone we know isn't hospitalized, sick, or having joint surgery. Hardly a day passes without being reminded that none of our bodies are impervious to the effects of time. Too often we find familiar names in the obituary section of the paper. Phone calls begin with "How are YOU?" Not too long ago, the response would be, "Oh just fine, how about you?" and that would end the "health" dialogue. We did not hurt, so we weren't concerned. But time ticks forward. To become ensnared in our own aches and pains can distort our rational thinking. No one wants that to happen. But sometimes negativity creeps up on us without our even realizing it. Sometimes we are afflicted with medical conditions that can't be swept under the rug. Even as cognizant as we are about trying to ward them off, they happen. It is part of getting older, and it is part of the New Normal!

Our "YOUNG" friend Ken, sixty-five, had successful shoulder replacement surgery a few months ago. He seemed to recover well, and we all celebrated his welcomed mobility. A subsequent annual physical exam revealed his elevated PSA count requiring a biopsy. After shoulder surgery and prostate procedure, Ken was given heavy doses of antibiotics, designed to handle any resulting infection. Suddenly, on the eve of his departure to Seattle to visit a newly born grandbaby, Ken was rushed to the ER in the middle of the night. The diagnosis was startling. Not only did he have sepsis, a serious infection of the blood stream, but he had C-Diff, a brutal intestinal infection. He became very sick very fast, suffering extreme fatigue and zero tolerance for solid food. For several days he lay in the ICU, doctors testing and probing, as Ken's white count fluctuated. Optimistically, his wife Bonnye said, "We are not canceling our Seattle trip, because Ken will be better." How very much she wanted him to be healed. How easy it is to hope for a quick cure, and how hard it is for us to accept reality. And how terrifying it is for any wife to watch her spouse lie on a hospital bed, his weakened body assaulted by tubes. How hard it is for a wife to accept that suddenly she and her beloved have been thrust into a new normal. Getting older changes what we used to take for granted. Ken is at home now, and doctors have said it will take many weeks for his body to regain its old strength. Seattle trip is on "the back burner." "Life might begin at Forty," but the NEW NORMAL begins when older age slams our complacency and dispels the illusion that we are invincible and in charge of our medical wellness. Mortality is real, not a myth.

John and I each had our own wake up call when I was sixty-eight, and he was in his late seventies. For me, a non-athletic type person, walking has always been my "thing"... I adore being outside, feeling the pavement under my feet, ticking off the miles as I explore and revisit beautiful country roads. The endorphins surge. It is a savored opportunity to communicate with myself, to process thoughts, to let go of worries, concerns, and to return home feeling refreshed and energized. It is a great opportunity to be alone, walk those miles, practice my mantra of "Let go, let God" when life's problems feel perplexing. Virginia is a good place to live: experience the beauty, even the dreariness, of changing seasons: a constant reminder of the miracle of nature. Inclement days when walking is impossible are far fewer than they are "up north."

In 2006, shortly after we built our second and LAST Happy Ever House, our next-door neighbor asked me if I knew about Life Line Screening. "It's a mobile unit managed by trained medical technicians that travels nationally," Reny explained, "offering people an opportunity to have their arteries checked by a Doppler machine for blockages or aneurysms." Many of us have seen ads in our local newspapers or received notices in the mail that a Life Line Screening opportunity will be available. For John and me, I always tossed the postcards into the trash. Because we each faithfully subscribed to regular annual physicals, I assumed I was being well monitored. Our new neighbor told me about another much younger neighbor who took the test, a blockage was discovered, and surgery was required. This resonated. I told John, and we signed up.

I will never forget the morning of August 1, 2006. It was a perfect summer day, and as usual I took our little dog Molly for an early morning stroll in the sunshine. Funny. I remember saying a silent prayer that the Life Line Screening would go well. In the back of my mind, I felt niggling apprehension. A big medical day, for that afternoon my annual physical was also on the calendar. Having been a former smoker during our moves, and being treated for high blood pressure (a tendency inherited from the maternal side of my family), I worried. But, I was not overweight, had stopped smoking many years earlier. After the screening, the nurse finished my test and said, "Please take a seat over there." I was the only one assigned to those chairs. Soon another nurse approached me and said, "We believe we have just saved your life. You have significant blockage in your left carotid artery."

Stunned! I could not believe my ears. The expression on the nurse's face left no doubt she was quite serious. So, I promised to call my doctor, and I drove home in a shocked stupor. John stayed calm, but my heart was racing. When I told our (now former) primary care doctor about the morning's experience, she was very dismissive. "I don't believe in those tests." "Well, the nurse scared me to pieces," I replied. "And John and I are due to fly to Europe in a few weeks, and we need to find out more." Reluctantly, the doctor made an appointment for me to have the Doppler redone at the hospital that afternoon. At the end of that test, the technician announced, "You cannot leave here without making an appointment to see a vascular surgeon." By that time it was five o'clock. I quickly called my doctor of record, who said, "What do you want me to do? It is five o'clock." But, next day she did make an appointment for me to see a specialist, halfway to Washington!

En route home from the hospital test, I called my dear friend Martha whose husband had undergone two vascular aneurysm surgeries. Immediately Martha said, "okay, I need you to call our friend Dick R, a cardiac surgeon, and he will help." Long story short, I hated to bother Dick, whom we knew socially, so John went with me to visit the far away vascular surgeon, who listened to my carotid, and said, "I think we will watch you for a year." My husband said, "That is not good enough. Isn't there another test you can do?" "Well, yes, but I don't usually recommend it." "Do it!" said John.

The rest of the story is that my life was saved, just in the nick of time. THREE guardian angels to whom I will be forever grateful, and love with all my heart are responsible for my being alive. First is Martha, who kept nagging me to call Dr. Dick, which I did on a Sunday afternoon. He couldn't have been kinder to me, talking soothingly when he perceived the angst in my voice. Thanks to Dick, less than 48 hours later I had an appointment with the best vascular surgeon in the whole city. Dr. Z looked at the test taken by the other vascular surgeon, asked me if I had eaten lunch, and calmly said he would see me the very next day to "fix that carotid." Thank God! Surgery revealed my carotid was ninety-nine percent blocked. If it had closed up, it could not have been fixed, and I would have either had a stroke or been a candidate for one.

Although this was serious surgery it was not considered "BIG" like open heart. But for our family, it was a traumatic event. It caught us all by surprise. None of us could believe that I *needed* life saving surgery. I didn't appear sick. How well I remember walking in a daze the week after the Doppler, ironing like mad the morning of my late afternoon surgery, and watching whatever mindless program was on TV. As our Connecticut son Sam drove John and me to the hospital, I scribbled a hasty list for dispersing my favorite jewelry to our children. Until this carotid crisis, I admit I felt "immortal," that the threat of death was far into the future, that I did not need to consider my own demise. I did not need to write things down so that if anything happened to me, our children would not have to make difficult, emotional decisions such as what to do with mom's jewelry or other personal possessions. That has all changed. I now have a list. Yet, even though several years have passed, and I seem to be okay, I will never, ever forget how terrified I was, how shocked I felt that someone as energetic as I was could have a life-threatening medical condition. And oh, how hard I prayed that I would survive and be able to continue my wonderful life on earth. I hoped that God wasn't finished with me yet.

As this flurry of fear surrounded me, I failed to see how much my unexpected crisis affected John. On the surface he feigned serenity. He gave me good hugs and maintained his quiet support. But when Sam and John brought shell-shocked-me home from the hospital, daughter Susie, arrived with her two children from Seattle to play nurse/homemaker. John's mood shifted downward. He adores our children, each one of them. But suddenly he became short-tempered, touchy, unsettled, and threatened by our new daily life, or in his mind, our "home invasion." Doorbells rang, food and friends appeared, and John's tolerance for the resulting confusion was palpable. He was conditioned to a predictable environment. He had progressed well in his acceptance of living the non-corporate life, but he wanted his home life back to normal. He wanted to decide his own schedule, he wanted me available to share our life as we had. He was not used to my being "out of commission." He had not considered the aftershock of this surgery in his life. And I did not comprehend how frightened both of us were. My mind could not absorb the possibility of my death, thus leaving John alone.

One day, after watching her dad's mood swings, Susie said to me, "Mom, daddy's problem is he is scared. He is scared he would lose you, and he just doesn't know how to deal with it." Good for Susie. She read the tea leaves well, and although I know these were a tough few weeks for her, she never faltered, she never lost her patience. She kept an immaculate kitchen, she played the gracious hostess with guests, she kept her sweet children busy, she anticipated and met my every need, and she was fantastic. She and Sam, by virtue of flexible schedules and their innate caretaking skills were able to fill an immediate, unexpected need for us. Their siblings, Allison and Charley, are just as gifted, but with different demands in their lives at that time, their immediate availability was not possible. Thus, the four siblings, in sync with each other, crafted a plan of action to help their far away parents, suddenly thrust into a new phase of life.

As I contemplate that life altering, frightening experience nine years later, I know even more the importance of listening to our gut feelings. When we sense something is amiss, we must be pro-active with our medical care. If our neighbor had not alerted me about Life Line Screening, if the Life Line Screening nurse had not put the fear of God in me, I might not have understood the gravity of the blockage. If I had succumbed to our (former) primary care doctor's dismissive attitude and not insisted on another Doppler test, I might have died. If John and I had listened to the first surgeon, I might not have had the surgery in time. And if my caring, beautiful friend Martha had not insisted, I might not have called our heart doctor friend, who in turn called his vascular surgeon friend who performed my life saving surgery in the nick of time. All of these events, all three of my angels, resulted in my prolonged life. I cannot waste precious time, and I can never stop being grateful to be alive. I also cannot hold back when I want to tell someone near and dear to me that they are special, that I love them, and that I count them among my dearest blessings. I cannot harbor any negative feelings for more than a few minutes, and I cannot hold a grudge. Life as we know it can change in a minute. Life as a healthy person is a gift. And, we have no idea how long we will "hold it gently in the palm of our hand."

My carotid blockage was a close call and a priceless lesson. Why? Because each morning of my life I wake up, say "Thank you, God," and feel enormous gratitude for being alive. It must be that "God isn't finished with me yet." I must give back all I can to thank Him for His divine mercy and my three angels for saving my life. It is my job to try to be the best person I can be. It is my job to keep learning and growing all the days of my life. It is time never to take anything for granted again.

While this is a very personal story, it is important to relate one more. This one is about John's close call with sepsis, a virulent infection of the blood stream. This event also took place in the summer time: August 2012. The week before the crisis, we were in the mountains of Virginia at our time share house with our older daughter Allison, her younger son, Seamus, and our fourteen year-old grandson, Brad, with us for his first solo visit from Seattle. Everything seemed just fine, except for John's occasional comments that his back hurt. Being the victim of chronic scoliosis, we did not pay attention. Instead we concentrated on enjoying each other and all the activities of the area. By Monday of the next week, the day we were to drive Brad to Baltimore for his non-stop flight back to Seattle, John announced, "I really don't feel very well." I dosed him with two Advil, and said, "we have no choice but to drive to the airport; I need you with us."

As we drove home that evening in the pouring rain, I knew John felt awful. But he kept driving. I thought he was stressed by the wicked drive on I-95 in the horrendous weather. As soon as we arrived home, we popped him into a hot shower, gave him a strong shot of Scotch, after which he said he felt better and could sleep. But, in the middle of the night he awoke shivering, with a high fever. He saw our (new) doctor the next day, who thought the back pain might be caused by a urinary infection. Dr. D advised me to keep an eye on John. By the next afternoon, John was burning up, in terrible pain, and it was obvious he was one sick fellow. Another call to our doctor, who promptly said, "take him to the ER right away. They will be waiting for him."

With a fever of nearly 104 degrees and being seventy-eight years-old, John attracted everyone's attention. Lots of fluids, lots of questions, lots of testing, an arsenal of IV antibiotics…I knew he was terribly sick, but he was responsive, surprisingly jovial with the nurses. Denial is a buffer. It keeps us from imagining the worst. At one point when the nurses were conferring about John's precariously low blood pressure, I piped up and sassily proclaimed, "Show him a picture of Barack Obama and that will do the trick!" My joke fell upon deaf ears, but John smiled broadly. Truth be told, in the wee hours of that night, I did not permit myself to realize how sick he was. I did not realize when his blood pressure dropped dangerously low that he was in septic shock. God Bless the ER staff for their competence. God bless the ER doctor who quickly suspected a tick bite might be the cause. God bless the ICU nurses for their many days of constant care, their loving TLC, their patience as I asked countless questions. God bless the infectious disease doctor whose aggressive testing and treatment saved John's life.

As I drove home about 2 a.m. that first scary night, I remember my hands shaking on the steering wheel. Feeling a violent wave of panic, I was terrified that something could actually happen to John, that he could be snatched away from our loved ones and me. The thought was too painful to ponder, so I flipped into denial mode. It wasn't until later in the week that three of my dearest friends who supported me those early days announced the gravity of John's condition. I guess I was glad I didn't realize it at the time, else I might not have been able to sit with him hour after hour, without non-stop tears.

John's health crisis was a bona fide brush with death. Only astute doctors with consummate competence, using comprehensive testing and powerful antibiotics were able to zap the infection. After ten days in the hospital, our infectious disease doctor calmly announced, "If John was in St. Petersburg (our planned fifty-fifth anniversary trip) when he got sick, he would have died. Russia's medical world is way behind ours." Thus, in a space of six years, each of us experienced a major medical emergency. Each of us faced our own mortality. Putting that reality into words is impossible to describe. We think of death in terms of other people. We "pretend" we are immortal. Eventually, however, we "see the light." Reality seeps into our beings and we realize how lucky we were to survive. With profound gratitude and humility we thank God for sparing us. Medical scares must not paralyze us. We must keep moving forward, cherishing each day. We must make wise choices, pay attention to any warning signals, and we must embrace our lives completely. We only have one chance to live on this earth. As Walt Whitman said, *"Keep your face always towards the sunshine…and the shadows will fall behind you."*

Grasping acceptance of life's fragility in the midst of frightening medical problems makes us stronger. For many of us these brushes with death deepen our faith, making us more sensitive to the feelings and experiences of those whose lives we intertwine. Maybe they make us BETTER, more loving people. Maybe they inspire us to give more of ourselves whenever we can. Maybe they just smooth out the kinks in our lives, smooth out the ripples of our hearts, and maybe they make us do all we can to be worthy of the second chances we have been given. It is hard to imagine anyone leading a meaningful personal life without faith, but we know many on this earth do. And that is their choice, as it is not for us to know the reason why belief in a higher power is not essential to their lives.....but for me, I can never forget the gift I have been given, the gift of a healthier life. May I cherish it for as long as it is granted. And I will always, always thank God with all my heart.

"Praise God from whom all blessings flow..."

Managing Our Emotional IQ in Older Age

Emotional health affects older people, too. Not just during the adjustment period of retirement. Not just as we downsize. But it can also surface in the course of our everyday life. Emotional health is a critical aspect of being alive. Recently I read that more older people are taking anti-anxiety drugs or anti-depressants than ever before. Why? I am not sure, but I am guessing it is partially because we are living longer, our fixed incomes stay "fixed," we are stretching our dollars further, and we live in an uncertain economy and world situation. We can't help but worry about what the future holds. Most situations are beyond our control. But it doesn't mean we are insensitive to what is happening. And it doesn't mean we are unaffected either.

One of my all time favorite books is called *Emotional Intelligence* by Daniel Goleman, who wrote this excellent self-help book in 1995. One section deals with "how medicine can enlarge its vision to embrace emotions.... two large implications of scientific findings must be taken to heart." The first way is "helping people better manage their upsetting feelings...anger, anxiety, depression, pessimism and loneliness".... One way is to develop a *"high payoff preventive strategy to teach emotional management to people reaching retirement age, since emotional well-being is one factor that determines whether an older person declines rapidly or thrives."* Wow, these are potent words! For decades I have felt that if we can manifest a positive attitude we can navigate our way through some awfully choppy waters. And when we can't, we need to seek professional help. Now, Dr. Goleman reinforces this thought.

Thus, as we adjust to our aging bodies, the need to pay attention to our emotional IQ should rise on our priority list. Although many of us remain unaware of its importance, we tend to blame changes that beset us on the mere process of aging. We sweep uneasy feelings under the carpet. After all, as we grow older, many of us feel most emotional turmoil is history. Careers are over or waning, children are educated and launched, and most of our elderly parents have passed away. For these reasons, we believe our lives are more predictable, and we are in control. However, some sixty year-olds are still working, taking care of their elderly parents, and some are even supporting older kids living at home after college. But everyone's life evolves. Older kids eventually move out, get married and start their own lives. By the time most sixty-something people reach the end of the decade, their parents have usually died and family responsibility shifts. They become the "older generation." Retired people begin a new phase, projecting the hope that their lives are simpler. Aside from coping with periodic health issues, many seniors are content to adopt a quieter, less demanding schedule. If budgets permit, they can hire help to do chores. They are free to fill their days with bridge games, knitting or TV, short walks in the sunshine, and easy meals. And if they are living in a retirement facility, they never need worry about a leaky faucet or fixing dinner. Simplicity on some levels, yes, but not always devoid of assaults on one's emotional IQ.

Funny, however, how busy we retirees can be, and funny how we still have the same feelings, the same ability to worry about concerns that may be different than they once were, but continue to affect us. Funny how no matter the ages of our adult children, we fret and stew about them, especially if something difficult is affecting their lives. We look into the mirror and we don't see the same faces we once saw, but our emotions still churn and create occasional firestorms in our hearts. Hopefully, most of us are able to "talk ourselves down" to dig back into what we once learned, resurrect it, and apply it to the concern we currently possess. But sometimes we need outside help. Professional help at any age is essential and acceptable.

Recently a wise and younger friend of mine asked me how I intended to cope if something happened to John. I looked at her, and said, "Wow, I don't know. I can't think about it." Rationally, however, I know the first thing to do is sell my house, and move into a retirement facility. That would be paramount. Even though many professionals say no one who loses a spouse should relocate during the first year, I would not want to remain in our favorite-ever-house without John. And, having no family in the area, I would need to move as quickly as possible. As for grieving, take it one day at a time. Grieving for an adored spouse must be unique and unlike any other loss. It has to feel as if a chunk of our heart has been sliced away with a butcher knife, leaving us bereft and floundering.

My soeur du coeur Linda, whose husband, Miles, died several years ago, told me that "without a strong faith and strong independent streak, living alone (after the death of a spouse) would be perpetual sadness, possibly self pity, as well. We have to be comfortable in our own company. Giving thanks for each new day, with open hearts and minds, helps overcome the loneliness." Linda's words are wise, revealing and touching…."perpetual sadness" equals profound loss. How admirable Linda's actions are that she knows how to address her feelings and to move forward with her life. She is exceptional because she never exhibits any negative feelings. Her faith has always been invincible and an anchor to all areas of her life. She is an inspiring example of a woman who reaches out and away from herself, and who pursues interests that keep her mind and body active. None of her three children live near her in Florida, but when she is in her Connecticut home, she is closer to New Hampshire and Boston where two sons and their families live. Interestingly, however, Linda has selected a retirement home in Florida where she will move by the time she turns eighty. She will sell her Connecticut condo, and live her life in the warmer climate. Like my widowed sister Judy, Linda has taken charge of herself, and is doing it well.

Watching other friends cope with spousal losses, we realize that each person does it his or her own way. Women seem more able to manage alone than widowed husbands. Why? Men of our older generation have grown accustomed to being looked after, having their wives cook for them and run the house. Truth is, so many whose wives die first, grieve, but find another woman to love and care for them. Men of my generation are not solo beings. Do they react this way because they are lonely or because they are spoiled? I suspect they are both. I will never forget meeting a college friend we had not seen in some time, and I inquired about his wife whom we had known casually years ago. With a puzzled look on his face, he replied, "You didn't know that Carolyn died several months ago from surgical complications? Now, I am remarried to a lovely lady who was widowed." As dear as this new wife was, it was a shock to know that our friend found a new life partner in less than a year. Perchance the couple met at church or she brought him a casserole when his first wife died. No matter, as long as they re-discovered genuine happiness. This story is not meant to demean people who remarry quickly. Rather it is a commentary on the compelling need some widowers possess to remarry. Interestingly, there is a feeling that the happier a marriage is the more eager a husband is to find a new wife. This particular couple created a meaningful marriage for many years before the husband died.

In all honesty, I worry more about how John would manage if I were to go first. He would not be a good widower. He can fix a sandwich, make pancakes, cook an egg, but that is about the extent of his culinary skills. He would not let himself starve, but he loves having me cook for him and wait on him. I hope he would not rush at breakneck speed into another marriage, but it would be selfish of me to ask him to remain alone or lonely. Truth be told, it is the younger retirees who lean toward marriage, as they envision many more healthy years ahead. However, as men and women reach their late seventies or eighties, few elect to remarry. If they meet someone to whom they are attracted, they live parallel lives, enjoy each other but don't marry. When I faced my carotid crisis, I was terrified for John who was a "young" seventy year-old. I worried about how he would cope alone, with all our children living far away. I was also unable to consider his dashing out to find a second wife, selfish as that might sound. If I died, I wanted him to think about our good years and to miss me for at least six months to a year! I remember sharing that concern with a surgeon friend of ours whose wife was critically ill. He understood what I was saying. He was comforting as I told him my fears for John. He also knew what to say to John to soothe him. He responded to John with medical facts about my condition, and he reached John on a professional clinical level. That worked for John, and it helped me, too.

No one can predict how he or she will react to the loss of a beloved spouse. No one can tell another how to feel. In theory, we need to be our own best counsel. We need to strengthen our inner core and be sturdy enough within ourselves to handle whatever curve ball is hurtled at us. Only some people have that ability. Faith in God and His plan sustains many of us, but even faith can be assaulted by fear. We can talk to ourselves, we can be rational and realistic, and often we can assuage our worries. We can try as hard as possible to be our own therapists. But we are not always successful, nor should we expect to be. That is why competent professional help, and if needed, drugs are in order. That is why older people, or even younger folks, need to admit when they are beset by emotional upheaval. It is okay to ask for help. No need to reject being pro-active for treating unexpected emotional reactions.

Years ago, my parents' generation considered psychiatry or any kind of therapy anathema. It was for "crazy" people. And sadly, many people coped alone, and unsuccessfully. When I think about my darling father who was struck down at age fifty-two by Parkinson's disease, I remember the disappearance of his once ebullient self. For a long time, no one in our family understood what was happening to him. My mother used to say, "Hurry up, Gil, you are moving too slowly." She thought he was being perverse. She had no idea his slowed pace was the result of early onset Parkinson's disease. I remember how angry she was when daddy scheduled his prostate surgery the day of my high school graduation. She was furious, and yes, I was hurt he wouldn't be able to share my big day; but I knew my father was frightened and needed the surgery. Little did we know at the time that Parkinson's was already a factor. No doctor detected it…not his long time internist or the urologist.

Soon, however, the disease reared its ugly head, and daddy's entire life changed. He became withdrawn and sad. For a man who gave of himself to others, he became a stranger. His once buoyant out-going personality disappeared. He was still gentle, he was still kind, but he was miserable. He told me, "I am a prisoner of my own body, and it is a living hell." He even lost his profound faith in God, which had identified him; he honestly felt that he did something awful in his life to deserve this disease. He thought God was punishing him. Oh, how I wish he could have been helped with therapy. I wish he could have received medication to relieve the anxiety and depression he felt. But not even his devoted long time internist suggested psychiatric treatment. I wish my mother had been offered help, too, because she was ill equipped to maintain the level of patience and understanding she needed to care for her once vibrant husband's swift and untimely decline. My sister was married and living in Milwaukee, and I was in college, and married after two years, subject to many corporate moves. So we were virtually no help to mother or daddy.

We all ached for him and missed his joie de vivre, his energy, and his enthusiasm. As the disease progressed, it enveloped him in a chokehold. And in the late 1950s and early 1960s the only remedy available for a Parkinson patient was phenobarbital (a mild sedative) or a daily drink of scotch, which daddy resisted, because of his aversion to alcohol. In today's world, drug or cognitive therapy might well have helped. I believe he would have accepted it, had it been presented as a means of coping with his illness. My sister remembers that daddy's impression of seeing a psychiatrist was tantamount to "going to the guillotine." But reason tells me that a man as intelligent, alert, and sensitive as my dad would be receptive in today's world. How sad to watch him transformed into a mere shell of his former self, both mentally and physically. I do believe daddy tolerated Parkinson's to the best of his ability, given the tools to cope that he had…he did not complain, he was very undemanding. But he never could understand why he was afflicted. Although the common belief was that patients who contracted the vicious flu virus of 1918 were susceptible to Parkinson's (and my father had the flu), my dad thought he had displeased God, and was therefore being punished. How sad he felt that way. He lived the Ten Commandments. He was a beautiful, loving, giving man. Research has proven Parkinson disease is not caused by that 1918 flu epidemic. We ache for men like my father but we are grateful for progressive medical treatment of Parkinson's. The benefits of psychiatric and psychological therapy for ill people have also escalated exponentially.

Even in this twenty-first century there is a narrow segment of our society that believes professional help is for "the wealthy," or for those "who cannot figure it out themselves." It is beyond sad, beyond devastating to think that anyone can delude him or herself into thinking that they alone have all the answers. It is a skewed perception. How do we teach others that no one way of living is immutable? How do we convince others that the only ones they hurt as they practice avoidance or denial are themselves and those they love? How do we convince them that they alone possess the power to change? How do we determine the origin of their beliefs? Maybe it is years of living with an undeveloped Emotional IQ, maybe it is years of denial, maybe it is years of "toughing it alone." Who knows? But I do know one late fifty something person who says his actions are a result of "how I am wired." On one level, he is smart, savvy, educated. But when it comes to psychiatric treatment or psychotherapy, he draws a hard and fast line. He resists completely. He rails against any professional advice or suggestions. He says that when a problem arises, "I sit myself down, and I say, 'self, what should we do?'" Maybe that is his answer. Maybe it makes him feel in charge and in control at the time, but when and if a real crisis occurs, will he still feel that way? Only time will tell. I hope he doesn't have to learn the hard way. I hope he doesn't ignore a crisis with a red flag flapping madly, signaling trouble, only to find that he was wrong not to take action. As for "wiring," it does not last forever. Even household wiring must be replaced. If we all adopted a rigid formula for our own lives, we would miss a glorious opportunity to develop into the human beings God intends us to be. We are meant to evolve and grow. One of the saddest qualities any human can possess is the attitude that "I have all the answers. I don't need anyone's advice, because I can do it myself. And I resent interference." If healthy Emotional IQ measured that kind of thinking, my guess is it would register barely above a zero.

My husband has a theory that those of us who are forced to accept change as our adult lives evolve are better equipped to adapt new ideas or new environments. Little children can be more flexible than adolescents or older people by virtue of their youth. When people stay in one place all their lives, they resist change. They have no experience living in different environments. Their homes are sacred to them. John and I witnessed our mothers' refusing moves to retirement centers at the appropriate time. I will always remember being sent to Cleveland to help my mother-in-law prepare for her "forced" move to Virginia. She was already in the throes of early dementia. My own mother died at home, but it was an abysmal last few years for her and her family. John's mother moved, kicking and screaming, from her beloved Cleveland to Virginia, but she never accepted her plight. She felt angry and betrayed. She could not realize that her older son, a respected medical doctor, wanted to look after her, have her living in the same town as he and his wife did. Even after Charlotte was settled into the assisted living complex, she tried to arrange a move back to Ohio. It never materialized, but she was resentful. Her Maine-Yankee determination kept her alive and snarky until she was ninety-eight years old, but only the sight of a visiting great grandchild brought a real smile to her face.

Old age and the decline of her mind and body were devastating to John's mother. For many years she mourned the loss of her youthful beauty more than one can imagine. And as a patient in the nursing home in the 1990s, she was often over medicated. John's attentive brother did his best to monitor her dosage. Without medication, she became too querulous to manage, often border-lining on violent. We ached for Jim and his wife Tommi as they were always the first responders for Charlotte's crises. We could not be good stewards of her care as we lived three hours away in Richmond. At least we could visit, and we did, but probably not as often as possible. The last years of her life were difficult in many respects, but they might have been worse if she were alone, with no nearby family, in a Cleveland nursing home. How grateful we are for medical advances, particularly in the treatment of geriatric patients.

Several people I know take a mild dose of Lexapro each day to control anxiety. One is a lovely neighbor much younger than I who told me that she takes the drug and that it is "essential" to her well-being. She is a vivacious outgoing lady, openly expressing gratitude for the pills: "I have been on them for years." Another friend told me that after retirement, he and his wife were both prescribed anti-anxiety pills. At first I was surprised, but then it made sense. This couple had sustained huge losses of control over their lives. Not long ago I encouraged a divorced friend of mine to tell her doctor about her mounting anxiety. She lived alone, had "all her affairs" to manage, and she was struggling. Happily, she listened, and her doctor prescribed a mild dose of an anti-anxiety drug. She feels better. I may not take a drug for depression but I feel reassured to have a prescription for Ambien, a well-known sleep aid, when needed, which can be often. Some people may disagree, but I do not. I remember hearing that those of us with a pre-disposition to high blood pressure do better if we are not sleep deprived. That makes great sense. Thrashing around the bed or reading half the night is not restful. It agitates one.

A word of caution based upon a real life story: people taking a pill to control anxiety or depression must be carefully monitored by a medical doctor. These drugs are not to be tossed around blithely. They ought to be prescribed in tandem with therapy, if possible. I know a young college girl who sought the advice of a doctor on campus because she was feeling overwhelmed and anxious. The doctor gave this lovely twenty year-old a prescription for a very strong dose of a drug called Sertraline. He then told the girl that if it didn't work, she could double her daily dose. How stupid. How irresponsible! Did the doctor ask the girl what other drugs she was taking or ask her to check in with him before she increased her own dosage? No, and as a result the young lady suffered adverse side effects, which do not disappear without time and attention. She also was not advised that once she began taking the medication, she could not take it randomly. To go on and off such drugs is dangerous: mood swings, irritability, and even suicidal thoughts can develop. Never take a drug at any age without knowing the effects it can have on the mind and body. It is frightening to believe that any campus allows a doctor to dispense drugs lightly to uninformed young people. Let us hope this scenario is not repeated around the country. Thus, no matter how young or how old anyone is, anti-anxiety or anti-depressant drugs must not be ingested like jelly beans. One can never be cavalier in drug usage.

So, what is a good prescription for older folks managing our own Emotional IQ on a daily basis? We must be alert. We must remember to stay aware of how we are managing our lives. We need to be as up to date as possible on medical advances. That is being pro-active and smart. In addition, for many of us, it might suffice to take a conscious inventory of our blessings. Perhaps we should remind ourselves of them each day. Perhaps we can take a moment to write an encouraging email to someone who needs a lift. We can think about and do for others. Perhaps we can even "change our channels" and lose ourselves in a book or a great movie. Maybe we can make a batch of cookies to share with friends or to hide in the freezer until we are caught in the clutches of the Cookie Monster. A great uplift for me is to play music CD's: classical, country, Broadway, oh... and yes oh yes, Dixieland, which will automatically make you want to kick up your heals and pretend you can still jitterbug and dance the Charleston!

This may sound naïve and rather simplistic, but it seems possible that if we can work through a scary time, we enrich our Emotional IQ. In the last many months I observed my husband manage panic attacks that have plagued him periodically for years. He saw an excellent cognitive therapist, learned invaluable breathing techniques, and the results are terrific. According to John, each time he feels himself approaching the early throes of an anxiety attack, he practices his breathing and manages to avert the problem. It REALLY works. He is to be celebrated for seeking professional help, to talk about his issues, to learn new techniques, and for his willingness to admit and address his problem. It took seventy-nine years, but he did it, and I could not be prouder of him. He is finished with his treatment now, but his doctor has kept the door open if ever John wants to return for a "tune up." Yay, John!!

Thus, regardless of age, never deny the value of excellent psychological or psychiatric help. To say that it is not for me, or it is only for rich people, or only for those who can't figure things out for themselves reflects an uninformed, ignorant attitude. Those people need to be educated and helped. They are at risk of suffering from their own deep-seated emotional problems. But as we all know, "Rome wasn't built in a day," so it is for those of us who believe in professional help to reach out and try to enlighten those who are left behind. We need to be loyal advocates of seeking help, and if the time arises when we make a difference in someone else's thinking, may we do it with sensitivity and compassion. Society has made infinite progress in the last six decades, and it will continue.

During our era of multiple moving I often felt overwhelmed. At three different stages of my life and in three different cities, I sought the help of a therapist. While I will never know until the time comes if I can manage every crisis on my own, I admit to moments when I crawl inside my brain and resurrect a thought or insight from one of those sessions. It has been twenty years since I had therapy, but the third and last professional I saw was a wonderful minister/psychologist who enlightened me more than I ever thought possible. To this day, I can hear Dodie's voice echoing in my head when the night terrors or unreasonable fears plague me. I remember her telling me to "talk to your tears, as they are a manifestation of fear or anger." I have never forgotten what she taught me. Many lessons were learned, and the messages were permanently etched in my mind. May I always give myself permission to remember and apply to the situation at hand. I know I am not afraid to ask for help, and I know that keeping my Emotional IQ as healthy as possible is critical at any age.

As I mentioned earlier, Daniel Goleman's *Emotional Intelligence: Why It Can Matter More Than IQ*, is one of my all time favorite self-help books. The subject matter is a fascinating illumination of our innate smartness. The front flap of the books notes: "Some of us may be born with a high IQ while others are born with a more modest IQ. These factors add up to a different way of being smart, and that is what Goleman calls `Emotional Intelligence,' which includes self-awareness and impulse control, persistence, zeal and self-motivation, empathy and social deftness." Reading the book is an uplifting experience. Although it has been many years since I have read it, I remember the simple tools I learned to assuage my own anxious or down days. Just as the childhood story of Pollyanna presented a girl who always looked at life on the bright side, Goleman insists that optimism through practicing the power of positive thinking does wonders for our emotional well being. He calls it the "great motivator." "*Optimism is like hope. It means having a strong expectation that, in general, things will turn out all right in life, despite setbacks and frustrations...optimism is an attitude that buffers people against falling into apathy, hopelessness, or depression in the face of life, providing of course, it is realistic optimism; a too-naïve optimism can be disastrous.*"

This book is for anyone interested in additional information or in bolstering his/her own Emotional Intelligence. It's a treasure trove of facts plus common sense insights into our own ability to elevate our moods, to become more empathetic, to raise healthy happy children, and to have a forever-successful marriage. This book also correlates the connection between a positive attitude and a healthy body. It may not deter all medical problems, but if it can make a difference in how we respond to illness or disease, then we owe it to ourselves to become enlightened. Many centuries ago a contemporary of Aristotle had this to say: "*The great end of learning is nothing else but to seek for the lost mind.*" And in 1780 wise Abigail Adams wrote her beloved husband these words: "*Learning is not attained by chance, it must be sought for with ardor and attended to with diligence.*"

Dating in the Elder Years

In May of 1968 my sixty-three year-old mother became a widow after nearly forty years of marriage. She was relatively young, and had many healthy years ahead of her. Although my father was ill with Parkinson's disease for more than ten years, and my mother knew his life span was limited, she was nonetheless bereft. How well I remember flying to Cleveland the day before daddy died. The next day we spent the morning with him in his hospital room. We were able to talk, and I remember my father's asking me when I had "become a blonde." I remember it was a cold, dreary end of May day, and I was shivering in my cotton skirt and sleeveless top. (Coming from Maine, I had packed for warmer weather in Cleveland.) It had been nearly one year since I had seen daddy. How sick and frail he looked. It was heartbreaking. When he called for the nurse, mother and I retreated to the hospital cafeteria. As we returned from a quick lunch and walked toward daddy's room, the nurse told us that he had died a few minutes earlier. We collapsed into each other's arms. My mother was devastated, and I was numb. Yet, in some ways I think she felt a sense of relief, as his care had been constant and enervating for many years, and the quality of his life was marginal. Living far away from Cleveland as I did, I was impervious to the grief that she must have experienced. I was too busy caring for three small children and dealing with the loss of my father.

Luckily mother was a plucky lady who did not wallow long. She tackled the tasks at hand. She took charge of her affairs, secured the professional legal help she needed, and never leaned on either my sister or me for advice or emotional support. Being an inveterate bridge player with a wide network of friends and acquaintances, she found solace in her hobby. Bridge was the link to her social network, and all during daddy's illness it had been her salvation. I remember her saying that her doctor advised her to hire nursing help so that she could travel periodically to bridge tournaments. Mother was a Life Master bridge player, several times over, so she knew her cards, and people sought her as a partner in sanctioned Duplicate Bridge games. It was through this association that she met a man named Bill who also was a strong player. They became friends.

Soon Bill pursued my mother, as he, too, was unmarried. She was a pretty lady, smart, fun, and a good bridge player. She also lived in a pleasant and well appointed home. The facts about his past were sketchy, and we were unsure if he had ever been married. He had one or two close relatives who lived in New Hampshire. He lived in a rented room in downtown Cleveland, seemed to be a loner, a pleasant enough fellow, not particularly motivated as evidenced by his sporadic career as an accountant. My sister and I were "luke-warm" about him, but we appreciated his kindness to our mother. He loved her cooking, and she loved to prepare dinner for him. According to her, he was "good company." Mother and Bill began to "date." Adamantly, she professed to Judy and me that they were "just friends," and there was nothing physical between them. It was not for us to judge. She was more than capable of taking care of herself. And mother was emphatic that even if Bill asked her, she would not marry him. Why? Because she did not want to change her last name or marry again. She still loved daddy. Little wonder. He was a beautiful man. For years, Bill was part of family celebrations whenever we came to Cleveland, and I remember his driving with mother to see us when we lived in Ottawa. I wasn't thrilled, but tried to be cordial. There was something about this man that struck a dissonant chord. In retrospect, maybe because of being twenty-nine when my father died, I couldn't fathom another man in my mother's life. And that was selfish of me. Bill loved to play bridge, as did my mother; hence the foundation for their friendship. She knew she was several years older than Bill, and she made us promise that if she died before he did, we would never print her age in her obituary! As life would have it, Bill died suddenly of a heart attack several years before she did. She was sorry, but her grief was nominal.

As my sister Judy tells me, "people come in two species after they are widowed. They are either in the casserole crowd or they don't want to be married again." And my sister, a lovely widow at age seventy-six, now in her early eighties, wants nothing to do with any advances made toward her by widowers. "My life is complete, with my family and friends and my own interests, and I don't want to worry about taking care of a man." Judy's attitude reflects that of other widowed female friends. My soeur du coeur Linda, whose husband was Miles, one of John's treasured college roommates, was widowed about thirteen years ago. She divides her time between Florida and Connecticut, not far from where two of her sons and their families live. Linda has never wanted to date. Once she told me a former acquaintance of Miles' invited her to lunch, and she realized he was interested. She was not! "Lunch was tedious," reported Linda. "That is the last time I will see him," said she. I admire Linda because at seventy-eight she still travels extensively, she takes her grandchildren on special trips once they reach age sixteen, and she, like my mother and sister, is an enthusiastic bridge player. Dating for Judy and Linda is not part of their agenda. They are secure within themselves, even though they are both great good fun ladies.

Most men are quite different, however. Those whom we know who have been widowed are not apt to stay unattached for long. I can name three or four friends who had very happy marriages but who tumbled quickly after their wives died. One friend who was married for nearly forty years and had no children joined Match.com. After a few months he met a lovely divorced, educated woman. They seemed like a good "match" but after four years of marriage, they went their separate ways. It was sad that it did not work. Perhaps after being successfully married for thirty-eight years to his first love, the happy memories were too hard to ignore. With the divorce behind him, this friend promises to move cautiously before he involves himself in another serious relationship. Perhaps if he had dated his second wife longer before marrying her there never would have been a divorce. It is never easy. There is always residual fallout.

Two of John's college classmates whom we knew well were widowed, and I can still remember being with one of the men at a Princeton Mini Reunion when he told me during breakfast that "I have been in love all my adult life, and I can't live the rest of it without being in love." His first wife had died of cancer, but within six months he reconnected with a high school classmate of his who had lost her husband. The two long ago friends began to see each other, and soon they were married. This was a "good fit," for both, and they shared several happy years until our friend became fatally ill and died. At least he accomplished his goal: he lived his life "in love" until his death. He and his charming second wife were happy, and they created many wonderful memories. She now lives in a retirement complex and is near all her children. To think that if these two people had not reconnected, they might have missed those special, happy, loving last years together. This thought makes the story even more touching. Our other friend whose college sweetheart wife died suddenly of complications following back surgery in her mid-sixties also found a wonderful widowed woman at church, and the two were most successfully married until his death last Christmas. The last few years were difficult, for sure, as his health declined steadily. Yet, through it all, their bond was solid, and they were blessed to have seventeen good years together. They also had little trouble blending their families, which may be because when they married all their children had their own careers, spouses, and offspring. Being wise and forward thinking, they chose to draw up a pre-nuptial agreement so that their combined finances were sorted out before they were married. A smart, sensible plan for older people entering second marriages.

To contemplate the thought of "dating" in the older years is impossible. For someone like me who has been successfully married for nearly fifty-eight years, it is anathema. I was four months short of twenty years-old when we were married. We loved each other completely. We thought that our destinies were inexorably intertwined. I remember telling my college roommate Kay that if I had not met John, I would have been "an old maid all my life." She looked at me as if I was goofy! Yes, goofy in love, and I intended to stay that way forever. When years passed and there were rough patches for us, we worked through them. Multiple moves because of corporate life were stressful, raising four children during that time of constant upheaval was demanding. And when John retired abruptly, we encountered more challenges. We each had to learn to accommodate the other on a full time basis. Seventeen years later, however, I only want one husband in my life. If anything should happen to him, then I would figure out how to create new meaning in my life, and it would not include marriage. I would not trade John for a winning bonanza lottery ticket or a night with Colin Firth!

Unless we "walk in those moccasins," it is impossible to know how divorced or widowed women and men feel or why they seek another partner. Of course loneliness must be a factor. Particularly true if a person is in his/her late fifties or sixties and anticipates a long life ahead. I understand why my mother enjoyed cooking for Bill, why she welcomed him as a bridge partner, and why she even enjoyed taking trips with him. Mother was vivacious and young at heart; both her daughters and all her grandchildren lived too far away for easy visits, and she was by herself. Independent though she was, it could not have been easy to sit alone night after night in front of the TV.

I remember mother's remarking that her social life changed after daddy died. Much to her dismay she was no longer included in dinner parties with old friends. She was seldom invited to "couples" outings. That seemed bizarre. Other single women say the same thing. One would think that if friends are close to each other, they would still seek the companionship of the one left behind. Why should a friendship be based upon being a couple? Are other women threatened? Are they afraid the widow will make a move on their husband? All this seems peculiar, but we hear it does happen. Hopefully our society is moving past that, and women or men who are no longer married are invited to parties and social events. My widowed sister is always included in activities with her couple friends, and she never fusses that she is ignored. Positive news! As we age, perhaps we worry less about someone's marital status. We simply feel fortunate to have good friends whose company we enjoy. They are rich blessings, and through them we may feel vicariously connected to the lost spouse, our friend, as well.

Asking a long ago divorced friend about her dating experience revealed some smart advice. Marion was quite young, still in her fifties, when her husband decided to leave. She knew they had challenges, but being a Catholic, she hoped that they could stay together. That did not happen. Eventually, Marion met a fellow close to her age, and they have had a strong bond for well over twenty years. He lives in Massachusetts and she lives in South Carolina. They talk on the phone each day, but only share periodic visits. They each enjoy their own families and their own life styles. This relationship, which has had its rocky periods, does seem to work for them. They are close friends. They love each other, too. Neither one has ever wanted to remarry. Thus, they continue as they are, remain devoted to each other, and live their parallel yet occasionally intertwined lives. Marion told me that her advice to single women is simple. "Be cautious whom you date. Check him (or her) out through mutual friends. If you live in a small town," says she, "it is easier to find out what this person is really like." But if not, "always go somewhere public, and always tell a family member or close friend where you are going."

One more thought about Dating During Older Years: remember to be careful not to confuse a need to love and be loved with a need to fill a gaping void in your life. My cousin Robin was barely seventy when her adored husband died after a long struggle with cancer. Her children were all married, and she was lonely. She says, "at that time, I would have entertained the thought of dating. But now, at age eighty-one," she says, "no way am I interested. I have my own life, and I am fine." Women seem to adjust to singlehood more readily than men do. As for a man marrying a much younger woman, consider this: if a man falls in love with a woman who is many years younger, he puts her in the position of one day becoming his caregiver. She should realize the risk she is taking. I think of my sister-in-law, twelve years younger than her husband. She was not only faced with being a young fifty-nine year-old widow, but the responsibility of caring for him in his terminal illness. She has missed him terribly and never remarried. Jim was the love of her life. A blessing, but also a curse.

Another scenario is the younger wife whose much older husband develops dementia and can no longer enjoy the life they both would adore to live. In many ways this could be the worst-case situation. How difficult to watch the once alert man slowly retreat into an unknown place from which he cannot return. Of course this can happen to either spouse. What about the woman who remarries, later in life, a man whose health fails and she finds herself widowed a second time? Yes, love trumps loneliness, and it prevails. But love in the older years should be carefully evaluated for all the potential pitfalls that can occur. Love at any age is a risk, but isn't it true that the younger we are, the better chance we have to love each other longer, to learn together and grow together?

In the twenty-first century our society is less tethered to the traditional constraints of thirty or forty years ago. Marriage is not always the solution for many people in love, especially if they are older. It is okay to be unmarried and together. A Florida couple whom we know met each other in their mid seventies. Both were widowed, in great physical shape, and they shared many common interests. They fell in love and now have a delightful lasting relationship. They are devoted to each other, but they also like their own space. Each retains a separate home. They date only each other, they travel together, and they admit quite honestly that this is the optimum solution for them. Why? Dating is easier and less complicated than marriage; and when we team up with someone who has lived with another person for many years, we each bring our own baggage, good and bad, to that new relationship. We also bring our separate families: children, grandchildren, plus our financial packages to the mix, to say nothing of our foibles. It is not easy to start fresh after so many years of marriage to one person who has shared many unforgettable milestones in our lives.

Dating for companionship in the later years rather than for marriage makes sense to someone like me, someone who has no first hand experience in this sphere of life, but who has learned lessons by the example of friends whom I trust and respect. Learning to live alone may be painful, but being true to thyself is ample fodder for the soul. The famous English poet William Wordsworth, whose words are without equal, wrote in his poem, "The Green Linnet": *"While birds and butterflies and flowers, Make all one band of paramours, Thou, ranging up and down the bowers, Art sole in thy employment: A Life, a Presence like the Air, Scattering thy gladness without care, Too blest with any one to pair; Thyself thy own enjoyment."*

Sex: The Elephant in the Room

Being raised in the forties and fifties, there was a three-letter word uttered only in hushed tones. It was a word that evoked little outspoken conversation and much solitary speculation. It was s-e-x. Many parents never mentioned the word in front of their youngsters, and fathers and mothers kept a tight lid on information about how babies were born or how they got inside their mothers' tummies. Fortunately, most public schools provided a basic course in fifth or sixth grades about adolescence, sex and reproduction. I remember receiving a thin book about menstruation from my mother. She told me the basics of what it meant and when to expect it happening to me. A talk about the "Birds and the Bees" was how the subject was addressed. I was also introduced to a very clinical description of reproduction, using all the appropriate terms, during a special health class in seventh grade. Lots of tittering by all the children as soon as class was over. A few were brave enough to ask questions of the teacher. I certainly did not raise my hand. I do remember comments from schoolmates such as "you mean my mother and father did THAT?" None of us were comfortable with the technical aspects of sex, and we could never imagine ourselves doing "it." When we went to a movie we shut our eyes when actors kissed on the screen, and we giggled uncomfortably if the kisses lasted too long. Nothing explicit was ever photographed. Instead the screen faded and the scene shifted to the next day. No rumpled sheets in the picture, no tousled hair, no showers and certainly no nudity at all. Movies never needed ratings because all love scenes were family appropriate. If a person was a certain age, much was happily left to the imagination. In retrospect, that subtle approach to romance was far more sensuous than today's version of love at the movies.

A few months after going to college there was speculation in my dorm about a girl named Diane who was bubbly, blonde, smart, and pretty. Too often she took a little suitcase with her whenever she went out on a date. Strict curfews prevailed, and we thought it was odd that Diane would take an overnight bag with her. "Maybe she doesn't have a purse, maybe she takes her makeup with her." One day a girl came running into my room and said, "Oh boy, can you believe that Diane actually goes to bed with some of her dates?" This news was horrifying to seventeen and eighteen year-old girls like my roommate and me. We liked Diane because she was fun and had a good personality. But the thought she could allow herself to crawl into bed with different boys was unthinkable. Her frank admission to friends that she liked to drink was also startling. The year was 1955, and morals were clearly defined. I remember quiet conversations among girls as to how we might change Diane's behavior. Of course, she was not the only girl who tumbled into bed with a date, but she was not like most of us. And admittedly, many of us were curious but prissy about the thought of pre-marital sex. That is not to say that boys didn't "try things" or that surging hormones for both boys and girls were not acknowledged and sometimes explored. But following through with those feelings was really unacceptable in proper circles. During my freshman year in college John and I were falling in love, but I knew my mother would kill me if I did not adhere to her code of behavior.

All colleges and universities had strict rules, too, about dormitory interaction of males and females. At Princeton, no women were allowed in boys' (it was not co-ed at that time) rooms after a certain hour. The guys called it a "No Sex after Seven" rule. One time John had to obtain special permission for his mother to be in his room after hours during a weekend visit. Proctors monitored the dorms on a regular basis, and God forbid a girl should be caught in any room. I remember feeling paranoid about visiting John's suite of rooms that he shared with several other fellows. What if the clock was wrong? What if my watch stopped? The best thing about this set up was that groups of friends could congregate, and the worst thing, besides missing curfew, was the frequent smell of dirty socks. Laundry was not a priority with these young men.

At Connecticut College for Women where I was enrolled, I will always remember one beautiful autumnal Saturday afternoon during my sophomore year when I was severely chastised by our housemother because I had the audacity to lead my friends and their dates upstairs to see our bedrooms. Because I was a dorm officer, I thought I was permitted to be a hostess/guide as long as there were several of us in attendance. I was wrong. Suddenly we heard the loud voice of the gray haired housemother who tromped upstairs and in a very imperious voice announced to me that I had broken the rules. No men were allowed in any dorm room without her presence. Duly scolded, I learned my lesson and never presupposed to invoke that privilege again.

By the time the sexual revolution of the sixties began, John and I were married and the parents of one darling little girl. We know that the desire for sexual fulfillment speeded up our marriage. We also knew that the threat of pregnancy before marriage was a huge deterrent to pre-marital sex. I had no option but to be a virgin bride. It was what was expected and yes, demanded of me by my mother. I loved John so much; he had his college diploma, and the thought of waiting two more years until after earning my college graduation was not appealing. He meant more to me than a diploma. Although I have never regretted marrying him, there is a wee small part of me that always wishes I had lived in an era when I could stay at the college I loved, earn my degree in English literature and be able to sleep with my fiancé, without incurring disapproval from my parents or scorn of my peers. In 1957 that was not meant to be. As the years have passed this regret has also faded. Now I feel I could hang a diploma on my wall for having successfully made our first ten corporate moves in twenty years while raising a family of four children.

In the last sixty years, attitudes about sex have changed radically. The birth control pill was invented, the morning after pill was invented, abortion was legalized, movies have become rated from G all the way to X. Talk shows interview people about almost any aspect of sex, and many children are born to parents who believe commitment is only important for however long the marriage is fun. It is sad to witness this change. It is sad to learn that girls as young as fourteen or fifteen are having multiple sex partners. It is sad to read how many junior high school age girls indulge in oral sex.

121

It is also sad to know that many young girls are being fitted for IUDs or given prescribed birth control pills while they are in high school or before they leave for college. But common sense mandates approval of medical precautionary action, as it is certainly preferable to teenage pregnancy. A girl who doesn't sleep with a guy may be dropped by a disappointed date, or she may even be subjected to date rape. She may be confused and frightened if she is expected to perform sex acts on boys who will forget her the next day. Without professional help, she may carry scars with her for the rest of her life. Too many underage youngsters have no idea what they are missing by not saving sex for later, when they are older and more mature. They may have no idea what they are giving away for free…without a wedding ring. Yes, for people my age, the pendulum has swung too far from the more appealing morality of an earlier generation. Surely there is a happy medium that does attract young people who are not swayed by peer pressure. Yes, I grew up in a rigid environment that would certainly repel many young people now, but to this day I have few regrets. It was easier for me as it was also easier for my friends, because we recognized the responsibilities of adult imposed expectations on us, and we honestly valued the sanctity of marriage. As proof of this statement, all of our close couple friends are still married to their original choices.

During the summer of 2015 a Pandora's box of disturbing sexual news was opened wide for the public to absorb. To say that it is revealing and in many cases destructive is an understatement. For example, a nineteen year-old prep school graduate was accused of raping a fifteen year-old fellow student girl as a school prank that went too far. Tradition invited student boys in their senior year to participate in an age-old tradition of inviting a younger girl for a kiss. Sadly relaxed standards and lack of vigilance by the administration created a very different attitude. The graduate was found not guilty of the felony assault charges, but convicted of having sex with a girl who was below the age of consent. He must register as a sex offender and will face some prison time. One can only hope that this case will serve as a wake up call for parents and school authorities everywhere to be more aware of what these young people are thinking and doing. Another fury unleashed from Pandora's box occurred when a website set up to facilitate sexual affairs was hacked, releasing the names and personal information for thirty-three thousand people who had signed up. Damage was swift and serious, with reputations, marriages, careers, and families being affected. Some people were so distraught they committed suicide. The reality "star" Josh Duggan's name was one released and he agreed to enter a treatment facility for help with his addiction problem. How horrific, how sad, and how predatory of website developers and owners to play upon the sexual fantasies of married folks. Dating sites, of course, have attracted many single people and many of those introductions led to marriages. But to encourage adultery - "Life is short, have an affair" was the site's motto - crossed the line.

Consider now the distressing trend that revolves around texting. This new approach offers "hook up" opportunities for young college age through twenty-somethings age groups. A participant does not need to submit any personal information except a picture that serves as the criteria whether a young person wants to choose this individual as a bedmate. No commitment is required, and in many cases only an hour of anyone's time is involved. It is merely a game for many young singles in different cities. They tally up their list of sexual conquests, and brag about it to their friends. Apparently this quick roll in the hay approach to life has replaced the old fashioned tradition of dating and courtship. Of course this is a broad statement to make, because we all know young couples who have met in college or during their single years, and have fallen in love and been happily married. Statistics say, however, that those young people who subscribe to the "hook up" mentality diminishes the percentage of successful marriages, and encourages the divorce rate which is already high enough among members of Generation X. There is a professor, praise be, at one Massachusetts college who conducts a course on dating for students interested in learning how to talk and interact SOBER with a person of the opposite sex to whom they may feel attracted. Kudos to this innovative professor. One can only hope that his classroom would be stuffed to the rafters with eager students.

The purpose of comparing traditional behavior during my college days versus some customs practiced now is to underscore the evolution of sexual conduct over the last sixty years. The fact that there are websites where young people can post a picture of themselves and invite any unknown stranger to view it and decide, "Oh yes, she/he is good-looking. Let's 'hook up'." Isn't this too bad? Isn't this approach to dating shallow, superficial, and irresponsible? Common sense tells us a person's face is hardly the sum total of the whole self. As the old saying goes, "Handsome is as handsome does." My generation finds it difficult to relate to many standards of today's youth, some of whom think that random, casual sex is a conquest or just another way to show off. There is a happy medium. Hopefully, before we seniors die, balance will be restored. I admit I am a poor one to talk about sex, which I hold sacred, but I also know that I still blink when I hear of youngsters living with one partner after another; and I wonder if they will ever realize the true meaning of love. Sex without love is a bit like making a sandwich without bread.

Since sex is never a topic of frequent discussion among our friends, it was interesting for me to learn from my dear *soeur du coeur* of fifty-eight years that as a Florida widow and resident she heard about a retirement area a few hundred miles away with a rather nefarious reputation. I searched the Internet for more information and found that this place is "the largest gated over-fifty-five community in the world. It holds more than one hundred thousand residents in an area bigger than Manhattan. And everyone gets around via golf cart…there are golf cart tunnels and even a golf-cart bridge to cross major highways." In addition to this unique feature, the community boasts the "highest consumption of draft beer in the state of Florida," and as of 2009 the *New York Post* labeled it the "ground zero for geriatrics who are seriously interested in getting it on." According to witnesses, sex in golf carts is not unique, and a black market for Viagra is thriving. In addition, and hold your hats for this fact: the retirement community is reported to have witnessed a "huge increase in sexually transmitted diseases." Yikes! And a similar report about another over fifty-five rambunctious retirement center is that women are reputed to have business cards printed with their names, phone numbers, and addresses. Apparently these ladies carry the cards in their purses or pockets, and when they meet a man who looks attractive, they pass along a card to him. That signals interest in "hooking up." Since people can move to many retirement communities as soon as they reach the age of fifty-five, it cannot be surprising that many singles may want to pursue their sex lives. Some may even find new spouses if they are divorced or widowed. But to be a promiscuous person eligible for membership in AARP is something hard to fathom. As the old saying goes, "We learn something new every day!"

Turning now to a scientific and comprehensive article in *The New England Journal of Medicine* has a calming effect. I read a fascinating piece called "A Study of Sexuality and Health among Older Adults in the United States." I learned that "little is known about sexuality among older persons in the United States, despite the aging of the population. Sexuality encompasses partnership, activity, behavior, attitudes, and function. Sexual activity is associated with health, and illness may interfere with sexual health. A massive and growing market for drugs and devices to treat sexual problems targets older people." Consider the TV airtime devoted to selling Viagra or Cialis and other solutions for erectile dysfunction. Apparently sponsors don't mind spending the money as they net positive results. And for many in today's world a product like Viagra is a gift of immeasurable value. The article also says that not much is known about sex among elderly people because few seek advice from their doctors. We are also informed "there is limited information on sexual behavior among older adults and how sexual activities change with aging and illness." The article told us that after the age of eighty-five there are only four men alive for every ten women, and that for women, the yearning for sex diminishes faster than it does for men. I love what a friend of ours once said, and this must be an old joke. He said, "I hope I live long enough to be shot by a jealous husband when I am ninety-five." Keeping a sense of humor is the key, no matter what age any of us is, right?

So, as we face the Elephant in the Room, we know that for every couple, for every person in their later years, they must decide for themselves what their needs are. They have choices, as we see, but they also have earned the right to privacy that defines who they are. We are hopeful that health allows us each to live active, vigorous lives as long as possible. But we also know that we are no longer young, and satisfaction can be rich and meaningful in a wonderfully close relationship with the person that we love. Sharing mutual interests, whether a concert, a sporting event, or a book to be treasured, along with precious time with each other and our families is something that eclipses all negative aspects of aging. One night not long ago when my husband was attending a meeting of fellow volunteers for a Mission project, I stopped for a moment to think what my life would be like if I ate dinner alone every night, if I did not have him to share a glass of wine with or a replay of our day. The thought made me gulp, and I reminded myself never to take our time together for granted. At any second, it can be snatched away. And for those of us who are married for many decades, there is no one else we know who can ever fill that gap. Our children are dearly beloved, as are our grandchildren; but there is still no one in this world who knows us quite as well as our spouses do.

Above all, may we each remember that sexual passion is glorious… but hardly the only cement that keeps a marriage vibrant. It is the flame that burns brightly for years. It nourishes our very beings; it fills a yearning in our souls; and it even helps to smooth over difficult passages. But like youth, it is temporal. Every one in this world evolves, physically, mentally, and emotionally… at different times and different speeds. Why else do some men or women weary of one partner and explore other relationships? Why else do some people commit adultery, even though they have little reason to transgress? Why are there so many divorces and speedy remarriages to younger women? Newspapers are full of stories about celebrities who flit from one marriage to another as people search for the perfect romantic alliance. Sometimes when he or she finds a new partner, they repeat the same mistakes of a previous relationship, and the new marriage has little chance for success. No one likes to admit that their bodies are changing even with rigorous workouts and exercise. The reality is their hormones are diminishing. Rather than chase a phantom phase of their former life, they need to count their blessings. The more years that we live, we older people get it. We are grateful for every good day that God gives us. We older people realize that life is all about change, all about accepting change and all about enjoying change that produces deeper and more precious feelings. We know that having birthdays is a "high class problem." If they concern you, consider the alternative.

Anniversaries: Celebrating and Contemplating

Anniversaries are a time for reflection. When we think about long-term marriages, and we think about those of us who have been lucky enough to share the majority of our years on earth together, we open a treasure trove of memories. Pictures trigger one's memory. We see ourselves morph from youth to middle age to older age, and we wonder how is it possible that time moves so quickly. In our master bedroom we have "The Brides' Wall." In the center of it is a vintage Bacharach photograph of my mother taken on her June 30, 1928 wedding day. My slender mother is adorned in her flapper style lace and satin wedding dress with cascading veil held in place by a wreath of flowers. Her bouquet is simple but full and round: stephanotis, Lilies of the Valley and trailing ivy. The setting is the living room of her parents' Pre-Depression Moroccan style home on Lake Erie. (My architect grandfather designed and built it, but was forced to sell the home and all of its beachfront property during the Great Depression when he lost his money.) There are large containers of daisies placed around the room. My mother's face, framed by her Marcel hairdo of soft waves, is composed, flawless, and demure. She was beautiful beyond description.

Above her picture is one of John and me as we walked arm and arm down the aisle of a Cleveland Presbyterian Church where my parents were married, where Judy and I were baptized, and where we went to Sunday School and church as we grew up. John and I look far less composed than my mother did, but we each glowed with unabashed happiness and youthful innocence. Susie's wedding picture hangs to one side of my mother, and Allison's to the other. Each beautiful beloved girl looked as radiant as she should on her wedding day. Also on the wall are the professional photographs of our two darling daughters-in-law, Joan and Stephanie, as well as our handsome oldest, first born grandson Liam and his sweet bride Natalie. When I wake up some mornings, I roll over and gaze at The Wall. Memories flood back, and I love to linger over each picture.

So many glorious memories, so much has happened in all our lives, and so many pleasures and joys have touched each of us. Of course, no one can live this long without having difficult stories to tell, but mostly we dwell on the good ones, as they are what count. We cannot stop but ponder how quickly life happens to each of us. If my mother were alive today, she would be 111 years old, and daddy would be approaching his 114th birthday. Our "bride" daughters and spouses are in their fifties, our boys and their wives are in their middle to late forties, and even our grandson and his dear wife are closer to thirty than to twenty-five. We remember when a year seemed like an eternity. Now a year zips by much too fast. Earlier this summer as I was writing a check at Fresh Market, I looked at the date. It was July 3. I remember thinking, "oh dear, once the Fourth is over, Labor Day is almost here. Why does summer go so fast?" No one our age wants time to zoom. No one wants to think about our days as numbered, and no one should be without a plan for the future. Much has been said in this book about retirees planning ahead. We know we must downsize, we must consider moving to a retirement facility while we are fit enough to be accepted, and to endure the rigors of the move. We know all the right things to think and do, but a few actions are a bit harder.

Some things are probably inevitable, such as the death of one spouse before the other, but such thoughts are buried deeply in our psyches. I know that when John and I had our narrow escapes with our major medical crises, we briefly thought about what we would do if something happened to the other. But it was never a thought that we allowed to take root. We each dismissed it as quickly as possible. Now, we are that much older, and all around us friends are losing spouses, forced to face the reality of grief and the future without their loved one, we need to address this unpleasant thought. We need to think about how we must proceed if and when it happens.

Recently John, who is his college class president for five years, term ending in 2017, told me that he has had several conversations with peers whose lives have changed dramatically, especially in their late seventies and as they each begin to turn eighty years old. He reaches out with phone calls to all who have suffered a loss. He learns so much about how these friends are coping. Two of his good friends living out of state lost their wives suddenly. One man, whose wife died of an aneurysm two years ago, seems to be handling the loss as well as possible, while the other says he "can't seem to makes sense of his life without his wife." Both men were married more than fifty years. The fact that their families are all around them is something that struck John. "How lucky these men are," he remarked to me. "All I can think is that if anything happened to you, I would have no children or grandchildren nearby. Even if I were living in Cedarfield, there would be no family." He is right. Friends are wonderful, essential to social interaction, and they do care. But they are not meant to be our on-call caretakers. "It makes a difference," said John. "My friend whose wife died last Christmas has both his daughters within a few miles of him, with grandchildren as well. At his advancing age he doesn't feel the urgent need to seek the companionship of another woman. The other has a nearby daughter who will be at his side as he has more cancer surgery. This business of being alone with no family nearby is something, Joy, that you need to write about in your next book." Now is a good time.

Perhaps addressing these thoughts has begun to stimulate an awareness that will implement action. As John tells me, "we need to think this through." He is right. We need to think it through how we will move forward alone, if and when we must. John and I know what it feels like to be long distance caretakers, but we don't know how it feels to be alone and the ones needing the care, emotional support and TLC. What we don't realize is that even when we move to Cedarfield, and if something, God forbid, should happen to one of us, we may have the physical care we need, but we won't have a chick or child living nearby to share our deep family history or lend the emotional support we will crave. This says something new to me, something I had not contemplated. What it says is that we seniors must always work harder to strengthen our own inner core, be stronger, less dependent, and more secure within ourselves. That should be a conscious process each and every day.

One thought occurs to me: could it be that those older people whose families are scattered around the country are far more compelled to think about what they will do if they lose a spouse than those whose families are within easy reach? It makes sense that for these people, like John and me, it is more urgent and critical to plan ahead, emotionally, for life alone than it is for those whose children live in the same city. I watch how well my sister has managed since her husband died. Yes, he was sick for some time and, like my mother, she must have thought long and hard about her being alone with three sons living in Japan, California and New York City....no one is close by. Judy is strong, she is self-assured, and she has no problem taking care of herself, making decisions and moving forward with her life. My guess is that like our mother, she never calls her boys and complains. She simply does as she needs to do. When Judy suddenly fainted for an unknown reason while dining with friends, she was scurried off to the hospital in an ambulance. A dear friend of hers sat with her in the Emergency Room. But, after it was determined that Judy should spend the night to rule out any serious condition, her friend went home. During that long night, with doctors and nurses coming in and out of her room, Judy said, "I thought a lot about mother and her being alone as she grew older. And I said to myself, 'You better get used to it, Judy.'" Happily all test results were negative, and she was released the next afternoon. My friend Naomi, whom you met in the REACHING OUT section, even at age ninety-three, is also equipped to take care of herself. She has a daughter living in Paris, another in England, and a son in New York City. AND Naomi lives alone in the house she shared with her husband, who died twenty years ago. So far, Naomi is extremely lucky as nothing (rap on wood) medical has occurred; but one of these days soon we all hope she will agree to sell her house and move to a retirement home...before something happens to her health.

We adore our children, and they lend us as much support as possible given the life styles they lead. Having his own business and being his own boss gives our older son Sam the flexibility to reach out from his Connecticut office on a regular basis to "The Old Guys." He is quick to pick up the phone, and hardly a day goes by he doesn't check in with us. Charley is great, too.

His job requires him to spend many hours in airports, and talking to mom and pop is a great way to pass the time. Our girls' lives and jobs leave little time for telephone calls, but they are good email-ers and text-ers. And our thoughtful daughters-in-law often check in with us. Truth be told, John's and my job is to prepare ourselves the best we can for living alone, for managing our own emotional needs, and for never being a burden, physically or mentally to any one of our children. We can do it, and we will!

So, what we are processing (thank heavens we are able to keep learning all the days of our lives) is that as these anniversaries come and go, we must continually remind ourselves that as comforting as it is to celebrate happy times, we must realize the importance of never lingering or living in the past. We can look at our pictures so full of memories in scrapbooks, in frames placed around our house, or on the Bride's Wall, and we can linger for a moment or two and smile at the past. But we cannot go there in any way except in our minds. We must keep plugging forward, learning, growing, and knowing that *"the one constant in life is change."* And change is something that will happen no matter how we fight it, how we wish it weren't an issue, and how we think we can avoid it. In 1951, Laurens Van der Post who was an Afrikaner and godfather to Britain's Prince William, wrote in his book *Ventures to the Interior: "Life is its own journey, presupposes its own change and movement, and one tries to arrest them at one's eternal peril."*

Duct Tape....aka... Hushing Mama!

A yellowed snippet of newsprint is taped to the cupboard over my computer. It says, *"Thought for today: Wisdom is divided into two parts: a) having a great deal to say and b) not saying it."* Something to read and digest each and every day!

DUCT TAPE for our family has become a euphemism for Mama's Hushing Up! For not offering advice unless asked, and for heavens sakes, not criticizing any action or anyone who might be offended! That applies to raising children, to our children raising our grandchildren, honoring their decisions, discussing religion or politics with a family member of a different belief, and so forth. Most of us older folks do learn that our advice is hardly important to anyone except ourselves... unless solicited... and, upon occasion, if we are asked, and if we are heeded, that is rare and marvelous. But, "to tell the whole truth, nothing but the truth," there lurks inside my naughty mind a huge urge to yank off the duct tape, once in a while, and let everyone hear how I really feel about some situations. But experience and reason mandate it is not a good idea. Thus, I do my best to behave whenever possible. There ought to be a special sign pasted over my computer to remind me to, as my friend Dr. Linda says, "DUCT IT UP!" Ask my wonderful daughters, and they will agree. But we understand and love each other completely, and we can talk to each other. Common sense says I have overstepped my bounds when a well intended advice email is not answered. I try to keep quiet about some things, but occasionally the words leak out. Silence from my girls tells me, "mom, you are annoying me, try harder." The message is received and acknowledged.

(As a quick aside: there is some speculation as to whether the correct spelling of the word is DucT or DucK...research indicates the more current version is DucT. So that is what will be used in chapter.)

Earlier in this book I alluded to this section. I mentioned that my mother was a fantastic advocate of staying out of her married daughters' business. Without realizing it, she practiced duct-tape mothering. She was such a good role model that I should have learned better. From the moment John and I were married, her philosophy was, "You have made your bed, now you lie in it." John and I, young as we were, did it all the right way. We never slept together before marriage, because my mother always told me, "If you do, I will know by looking at you!" I definitely believed her. John graduated from a top university with an engineering degree, I attended two years of college (in my next life, I will graduate) at an academically sound eastern women's college, and we had a luxurious six-month engagement period. We relished our blissful bride and groom time with festive parties, showers, presents, and lots of thank you notes. A week after his June graduation, John began his career with a large paper company. On September 7, 1957 we had the gorgeous church wedding, sanctioned by both sets of parents, with seven bridesmaids and seven ushers. I remember thinking that my wedding dress was a dream come true. We had lovely bridal photos, a sweet simple honeymoon, sleeping in one squeaky twin bed (I kept mints under my pillow so I would be "kissable" in the morning), on beautiful Lake George. One week later we moved to a paper mill town in upstate New York, a long day's drive from Cleveland. The rare times I called home and hinted that this move to rural Ticonderoga, New York was a giant adjustment for me, my wise mom said, "oh, Joysie, I must go stir the pot on my stove!" So, my mother was smart. She was an instinctive duct tape user, even all those fifty-seven plus years ago. She knew that John and I had to figure things out, make our own mistakes, lead our own lives, and grow up together. What a great lesson for each of us, no matter when or where we lived. I wonder if perhaps there would be fewer divorces now, fewer separations if more young couples had to rely only on themselves to work through their problems. Who knows?

Admittedly, without techie devices, such as email, cell phones and texts or Facebook, it was far easier for a parent to "stay out of it" than it is now. Although at critical times these cell phones are priceless tools, it is often true we are too closely linked. We practically breathe each other's air. Why else would the expression "Heliocopter Mom" be coined? In the 1950s, 60s, and 70s, our main form of communication was a handwritten letter tucked inside a stamped envelope; faithfully each week I wrote my parents our news, most of which related daily living. Rarely, we received a long distance call from them. Phone calls were a treat, and they were expensive. My sweet father was always at the ready with a "your three minutes are up" reminder. As generous a heart as he possessed, daddy hated phone bills…"wasteful spending." He and my mother, like John's parents, were survivors of the Depression with its painful memories and they forever watched "their pennies."

Duct Tape was a tape of the future, not yet invented, but my mother sensed when and how to keep her own counsel. Her "maintaining distance" in my young life made me think for myself, it made me grow up faster. And being only nineteen when John and I were married, my mother did me an invaluable favor, as she did my husband. We learned to lean on each other to manage our challenges. We talked things through by ourselves. And we always tried to follow the old adage, "never go to bed angry." We worked hard and established a firm foundation for our marriage. Of course, as often happens with young marriages, we hit some significant snags as years passed. John's feeling, however, is that we "grew up together." He is right. We did, and we had no choice. Life was challenging while we were raising four children, and multiple corporate moves consumed our lives. There were periods when we struggled to keep our compass on a steady course. But, with professional help and faith in God, we survived.

Actually, Duct Tape is good to keep at the ready most all the time. We older people think there is no problem we can't address with wisdom or no situation that we can't remedy. Just ask us! We think we have the answers, especially if a problem pertains to a grown up son, daughter, or grandchild. For parents who live near their adult children, daily contact is often the norm. Easy to know most details of their lives, but harder to keep the Duct Tape handy. Sometimes distance is a blessing. We, with far-flung families, cannot live in each other's back pockets, and we can't know every glitch that interrupts their lives. Ignorance can be bliss. If a child has a marital, job, or offspring problem, we parents may never hear details. That is okay, too. It prevents us from saying or doing anything untoward. In the last year, two of our offspring and one son-in-law suffered job losses. We gave moral support, love, and are always available to listen as needed. But, they worked through their own challenges, eliciting a positive effect. Out of pain comes growth, and out of growth comes wisdom. At this moment one of our nephews is separated from his wife of over twenty-five years. How hard for him and for his family, but perhaps a steady reminder that love and nurture is what he needs, as well as significant physical distance from relatives to provide him and his wife the space to sort out their lives.

John has a cute story about his paternal grandmother, who when asked which of her three sons she loved the most, she replied, "The one who lives the farthest away!" I could never love one of our children more than another, because to us, each one is equal, unique, and special. Yes, it is easier not to know every nitty gritty aspect of their lives. But oh how we would adore at least one of our chicks nearby, so I would have to practice the Duct Tape theory up close. Maybe I would learn faster that way.

In any relationship with an adult child or offspring, it makes far more sense to "accentuate the positive" rather than harp on the negative. Duct Tape is good for Grammys, too. And as I have said to daughter Susie, "it is lots easier to be a Grammy than it is to be a mom." So much easier for me to talk to my first-born granddaughter and give her verbal vitamins, even when her life seems a bit helter-skelter. It is much easier for me to dispense praise or even an occasional admonishment than for her mom, because it is not my job to raise this lovely young woman, to pay for her college education, to fret about her grades, her social life or work schedule, or to provide her spending money. My job is easy. Being a grandmother is fun. We can share meaningful time with our grandchildren, spoil them silly, and give them back to their parents. But, just maybe, we can imbue them with essential values without their realizing. We can (try to) be good examples, we can give endless love, and we can teach without preaching. Being a grandparent is the loveliest role in family life.

Occasionally families have multiple events colliding at once. This has happened to us, and it has gradually occurred to me that I must apply the Duct Tape rule when writing emails.

As I have already said, being too direct in an email can get me into trouble as my words emerge spontaneous and uncensored. How easy it is to sit at the computer and let thoughts and advice flow freely. I love to write; I feel emboldened and find my best voice when expressing thoughts on my Apple, with the "delete" key available. But, saying what I think in an email is really no different than saying out loud and in person what I think without the advantage of Duct Tape. So, as an adoring mother, grandmother, and now great-Grammy, I must be more mindful that as wise as I hope I am, my words must be measured and sensitive in the eyes of the loved one reading them. I do appreciate that John and our adult kids feel secure enough to tell me when I overstep my bounds. This doesn't happen often. But when it does, it is warranted. Amazingly, I have learned to accept their advice, and to be more gracious about receiving it: that is progress. Years ago criticism reduced me to a puddle of tears. Fortunately, we do evolve, and older age has its pluses.

Sometimes we Duct Tape advocates need to rip it off and take a chance that what we say might help someone we love. I can think of an instance where I stayed muzzled like an attack dog until I decided that perhaps, just perhaps, my words might be valued. This happened with a member of our family, enduring a critical time in his young life. He casually listened to those nearest him, but he refused to take action on a positive level. Sometimes being older is an advantage. And as the grandmother of this precious young fellow, I woke up one morning and thought, "Enough already," I have a perspective that no one else here has, and I am going to risk it and write it all down. I did, and now the reaction was positive. Do I think this would happen very often? Not really, but sometimes we must follow our best instinct, and let it all out. To write with love and lack of judgment is critical, but to say what consumes our heart, is essential. We do gain wisdom and experience with age, and we older folks must not be discarded into the trash heap of unimportance.

Duct Tape has usefulness in other areas of our lives. For example, who wants to be around a Know-it-All person who "stuffs" any listener within earshot full of mindless information...or who fails to recognize conversation goes two ways....or who appears to prefer the sound of his/her own voice? No one does. As a child I remember dodging Uncle Paul because he would talk on and on about seemingly nothing. He never asked anyone questions. It occurs to me that perhaps some older people become "stuffers" out of loneliness. Maybe so, but maybe they don't have enough to keep their minds active, they don't read enough. Thus, they settle into a sameness that does not stimulate their minds. Maybe they let their worlds shrink to accommodate the small space in which they live...maybe they let their attitudes suffer, their aches and pains rule them, and their lifetime disappointments overshadow their blessings. Maybe living alone without a community of other people is at fault. Maybe moving to a retirement home is important not just for the sake of one's physical well being but for the sake of one's continuing emotional and mental development.

Recently I attended the funeral of a venerable ninety-one year-old member of our church, who selflessly gave to the church for over fifty years. A veteran of World War II, the Korean War, two good marriages, Bob served our church well into his eighties as a consummate caretaker of the building, erected in 1915. He was on the scene when the boiler broke or the roof leaked. He followed the repairs through from beginning to end, even if it meant climbing up on the roof himself or sitting with a sputtering boiler until help came. Sadly, Parkinson's disease afflicted him. Bob's body became like a pretzel, bent in half, but still he loved to attend worship service, and he always greeted everyone with the quiet dignity and lovely manners that defined him. I remember one day seeing him and telling him how wonderful it was to have him with us. Stooped as he was, he paused on his walker for a minute, and said, "Oh, it is Joy! Good morning!"

The point of this story is not to say Bob was an advocate of the Duct Tape theory of life, because I do not know. I do know, however, that as smart and seasoned as he was, he never inflicted his knowledge on others in anything but a positive way. He was never tedious. He could be impatient if repairs were not to his specifications, but that was okay. He was a perfectionist, never spending the church's money frivolously. AND, he was always interested in the other guy. When his physical condition deteriorated, we heard our young minister say he had learned not to sit down to talk to Bob, because Bob wanted to stand up from his wheel chair, shake hands, and greet his visitor. Only then did they sit down... Pope John Paul II once said, *"The worst prison is a closed heart."* Bob's heart was always open, always gentle, and always engaged.

Keep the Duct Tape handy if you find yourself absorbed with the subject of aches and pains. Everyone our age has them. Be wary of fretting about something over which you have no control, such as The State of the Union or the Middle East turmoil. How easy it is to do, and how guilty I feel whenever I leap up on my soapbox. However, as a bona fide political junkie, it is often quite difficult not to espouse strong opinions. These days we live in a partisan country. Whether this condition is caused by media overload or an unbecoming tendency toward negativity, we must watch ourselves. When we are with those of like mind, it is okay to spout off, to discuss, to ponder the World Situation or hypothesize as to what will happen next. We can even discuss presidential candidates in a civilized fashion. To annoy anyone of a different persuasion is to blast off with one's own political dogma. In a bombastic, tedious tirade... OOPS, not good. Ergo, time for Duct Tape.

My husband also has very strong political beliefs. Luckily we are on the same page about most issues, but it about drives me bonkers when nightly news is on TV in our kitchen, and I am fixing dinner, and he interrupts and starts swearing at the poor news broadcaster. Sometimes, John is quite amusing, but sometimes he is bothersome. He talks when the commentators talk. When I have mentioned this to some friends, they, too, admit their husbands can be insufferable while watching the news, and many often change the channel at will. Is this a guy thing? Maybe, but although it can be funny at times, it is a Duct Tape moment in my mind. Just quiet...As the old saying goes, *"If you can't stand the heat, get away from the fire!"* Move your body to another room and hush your mouth.

So what we are realizing is that symbolic use of Duct Tape is critical to living happily as a successful retiree. Duct Tape makes us think first before we speak, before we offer unwanted advice, or before we plunge in and bore someone with unwanted information. Have you ever noticed a listener's eyes while you are speaking? Fascinating! The eyes tell it all. The look, the blank stare, or the faraway glaze reflects a listener's unspoken response. I love the words of Carl Jung who once said, *"The meeting of two personalities is like the* contact of two chemical substances: if there is any reaction, both are transformed." But, if there is no reaction, the contact is nil, and senseless, idle words are wasted on the listener.

We all know people who share vivid details of their day, even down to how many peaches they bought at the super market. There are those who talk ad nauseam about all the wonderful, spontaneous times they have with their children and grandchildren. The listener may be someone who may not have grandchildren or even family living nearby. Definitely a time for Duct Tape: it is a given that we each love our families, but it is not a given that we have families near enough with whom we can dash out to lunch or see on a moment's notice. And unless one is a grandparent oneself, to listen to the accomplishments ad infinitum of another person's grandchild makes for tedious chatter. However, if *asked* about how some child is, well, that changes the dynamic, and it is okay to yank off the Duct Tape and give a quick description. But for heavens sake, remember this little prayer, sent by a dear friend to me via email: *"Lord, keep your arm around my shoulder and your hand over my mouth!"*

On February 5, 2015 our first great grandbaby was born, a positively euphoric event. John and I were elated beyond belief, like all brand new great grandparents are permitted to be. I was so besotted that I mass emailed the first picture of this precious little fellow to friends near and far. Was that okay to do? Yes, because this was a monumental event that we hope all friends would want to share. But is it okay to send daily email pictures of baby dumpling Declan? No, it is not because I don't want anyone to say, "oh Lordie, here comes another picture from Joy, who can't stop bragging about this baby." Being sensitive to the reactions and needs of others is very important and a critical reason to keep Duct Tape handy at all times. Reading the expressions in other people's eyes mirrors how well or poorly our words are received. Staying mindful of the importance to be interesting rather than monotonous is a worthwhile endeavor as we grow older. We can always strive to be better conversationalists. We can keep up with the latest best sellers, award winning TV and movies, sporting and current events, etc. We are each our own unique selves, but we are always capable of listening and learning...and doing better!

To quote Carl Jung:

> *"The great decisions of human life have as a rule far more to do with the instincts and other mysterious unconscious factors than with conscious will and well-meaning reasonableness. The shoe that fits one person pinches another; there is no recipe for living that suits all cases. Each of us carries his own life-form...an indeterminable form which cannot be superseded by any other."*

Sharing Precious Friendships

When one has lived many years, one has the luxury of long-term friendships. Some of these begin during our early years, and some are formed at different stages and phases of life. We develop strong bonds. Friendships like these are circular. They are all about giving and receiving, and they enrich our perspectives. They deter us from being self-centered and absorbed in our own lives, they keep us focused on listening, learning, and expanding our minds. Why? Because true friendships must be nurtured in order to flourish. Just as a garden needs water, and children need good diets of love and proper nutrition to grow, so, too, do friendships need special, meaningful care.

A life-long or long-time friend is rare, and inexorably interwoven into our lives. Shared history does much to increase that tie. I am convinced, however, that precious friendships can be built not only because of shared history, but also because of deep-rooted common values. These friends touch a core part of our hearts. Through spending quality time together, discussing personal philosophies, observing reactions and sharing thoughts, these friends become far more than casual acquaintances. They achieve *closest* friend status. The older we grow, the more we seek out those kinds of friends. Most of us are no longer "into" the cocktail party scene with its signature idle chatter. We have outgrown that time of our lives. We don't want to stand up for long periods of time. We aren't interested in trying to impress anyone, and we prefer to spend time with those with whom we have many things in common. We like how we feel when we are with them... we learn and we grow. Later on, we will examine what happens to us when this kind of friendship takes root and flourishes.

Sometimes friends appear in our lives via shared activities. We like these people, and we enjoy them. These contacts may be important to us at the time, but when we move to another city or when our paths lead us in different directions, we gradually lose touch. As a result of our dozen corporate moves, I learned that although I genuinely responded to many people I met, I simply could not keep up with everyone. Not only did their lives evolve, but because of our moving to another city, our paths no longer crossed. In the first few years, we exchanged Christmas cards, and eventually, even sending Christmas cards stopped. And by virtue of time and circumstance and distance, these friendships disappeared into the ether. These fall into a category of "casual" friendships, and we appreciate the fact that they have nourished us a short time.

Nothing wrong, nothing unusual, merely a fact of life. It is just how things happen. Have you ever seen someone with whom you worked on a committee after not having seen that person for a long time, and suddenly, you are at a loss for their name? You know their face, you know that once upon a time you liked them, but doggone it, you can't think of their name? When that happens to me now, and I somehow remember that person's name, I approach him or her and say, for example, "Hi, Carolyn, I am Joy Nevin." The other day at the post office, I saw the woman named Carolyn with whom I served on a theater board many years ago. She passed by me as she walked into the post office, and neither of us spoke. BUT! By some miracle her name popped into my mind! As she approached her car, parked next to mind, I smiled at her and started to greet her, but I could tell by her expression, she had no clue who I was. Then I introduced myself. We had a brief, pleasant exchange before we each hopped into our cars. I was glad I spoke to Carolyn, and even happier that I remembered her name. Maybe these people were once "good pals" but they, as do we, move on...Life happens. We "like" each other, but we move to the next stage of life, and the loose tethers of the relationship float away. I do, however, believe that even fleeting friends leave a handprint on our hearts. Some acquaintances leave significant impressions. Each of these connections helps to enrich us in some way. Hopefully we have done the same in return.

What magic makes a really, really close friend? Chemistry! You know how it feels to meet someone, to feel comfortable with that person, and to be eager to spend more time with him or her. Shared values...but to know them, you need to know the inner person. Having lunch and chatting about superficial subjects can be amusing and fun, but how readily does the experience reveal the deeper level of that person? Some people don't want anyone to see into their souls. Some people are not willing to share their feelings. Some people just want to "keep it light." They wrap themselves up tightly so that no one has a chance to see what makes them tick. When we first came to Richmond from Connecticut, I was surprised by the difference in southerners and northerners. Everyone was very polite, but I was startled to meet new people and immediately be asked, "What does your husband do?" Not, what about YOU, but what about HIM! I was NOT used to that, and when I told John, he said, "Just tell them that I am a crane operator!" Silly John, but he knew exactly what I was saying. Now, nearly twenty-five years later and twenty-five years of knowing "southern" people, I can honestly say that we have made some of our closest friends.

Waaay back, in 1957, when John and I were first married and living in Ticonderoga, two ladies impacted my life. The first was our land-lady, a wonderful woman, a widow, mother of six children, who was only about twenty years older than I, but who quickly surmised how terribly young and naïve I was. Peg tucked me under her wing, was very kind to me and to John. She taught me how to iron John's shirts, she taught me about babies when Allison was born, she taught me many wonderful things, but mostly she taught me the necessity of growing up. At barely forty, she was not only a widow running a small restaurant and hotel, but she had survived a lethal house fire that killed her husband and one of her daughters. Peg cared for her remaining children, her aging mother, and managed to keep herself positive, with "cup half full attitude." In retrospect, I know that Peg was sent by God to be my mentor. She died when she was barely sixty, but I can honestly say, she was a close and precious friend when this ignorant young bride needed her the most.

And then there was Maid Marion who moved to Ticonderoga with her young engineer husband the same time as John and I did. Marion is my first and best forever friend from early corporate years. She is four years older than I, a teacher, a gourmet cook, a reader, a loving wonderful human being. Her life has dealt her nasty blows, including her husband's running off with a local Ticonderoga mother of several children, followed by his divorcing Marion and marrying that woman, surviving a (successful) battle with breast cancer, two knee replacements, a terrible car accident involving one of Marion's twin daughters leaving the child mentally impaired, and the list goes on....But throughout these last fifty-seven years, I always knew that Marion's and my affection and respect for one another have never faded, and even though we haven't seen each other in years, we have a bond that is made of cement. When we talk on the phone, we go on and on for at least one hour. Marion tells me what is on her heart, she shares herself, her joys and concerns, and we listen and learn from each other. That is what a real friendship means to me.

How lucky I have been in my long life! Nearly each place we have lived, I have found close friends whom I will always love. Sadly, some have died. It is where we are at our stage of life. Among the most memorable meaningful friendships came from our Wilton, Connecticut move which was, I believe, our tenth or eleventh move in the first twenty years of our marriage. Even for hardy corporate life-ers, our number and frequency of moves ranked high. At one point, we moved three times, with four young children, in thirty-six months! We owned three houses at the same time, and the company did not support any incurred financial costs except the interest on our mortgages. Our belts were scrunched in tightly. But we survived...barely. We had no choice.

Twelve years in Connecticut was not only a glorious place to settle after years of small mill town living, but it was the longest time our family spent anywhere during our children's growing up years. That USED to be my most favorite place. Now, I suspect it is number two....with Richmond being number one. Wilton, Connecticut from Mobile, Alabama occurred when John was barely forty-one and I was thirty-eight. Allison was a rising junior in college in the Boston area. The hardest part of this move, however, was moving Susie from Mobile in her junior year of high school. Her sister Allison had moved from Livermore Falls, Maine to Mobile, Alabama in her junior year as well. A drastic culture change! We felt brutal moving Allison from Maine to Mobile. She loved Maine...and the small town ambience and friendliness suited her. At school she was a sophomore class officer, a top student, and indeed "a big fish in a little pond." Going from a rural high school to an elite private school where joining a sorority was expected was foreign to her. She tried so hard to adjust, but her heart ached for her Livermore Falls friends. During one school vacation we flew her best friend Brenda from Maine to visit. That helped, but how well I remember the shock on Brenda's face as she was introduced to life in the south. Total culture shock! As I say in *Get Moving,* "the eleventh commandment should be, 'Never Move a Child against their will after their freshman year in High School.'" Wilton was a jolt to Susie, as she had grown fond of Mobile. To her credit, she soon made friends, and it was there she met "the boy next door," to whom she is now married some thirty years later.

One of the best aspects of living in Wilton for many corporate transfer families was the existence of Newcomers' Club, which welcomed all wives moving to the town. At first I resisted but eventually neighbors convinced me to attend a lunch. Eventually I was asked to be president of the club. "Why, me?" I asked? Because I was the proper age of forty, one of the nominating committee members had vouched for me, and they had run through their list of obvious candidates. I surprised myself by saying, "Yes, I would love to accept."

This turned out to be the best decision of my Wilton life, because through the club, and especially the board of officers, I met three awesome ladies, with whom I formed lasting and permanent friendships. Sally and Elaine were older than Betty and me by eight or nine years. We each came from different parts of the country to Wilton, although Sally and I had spent our early years in the Cleveland, Ohio area. Betty was our adorable youngest...from Pace, Mississippi. She married her college sweetheart, George, a Mississippi State honors graduate, and the two of them moved often and well with IBM. (In those days, IBM was known as "I've Been Moved" corporation, and adjacent to its Armonk, New York headquarters, it was rumored there was a sanitarium for wives with mental problems resulting from multiple moves.) Elaine came from Illinois, the mother of four bright and gifted girls. The four of us were mothers of fifteen children of varied ages. We were each the "original" (ie, "trophy") wife, and we all became members of the same glorious historic Congregational Church in Wilton. Thus, not only were we bonded by Newcomers, but by church activities as well.

When you think back as to why we form close friendships with others, we can't always pinpoint the precise reason. But over time and upon reflection, the pieces of the puzzle fall seamlessly into place. These women and I bonded because we were each willing to share stories, experiences, feelings, and emotions with each other. We were vulnerable because of the constant upheaval we had experienced. We needed each other, we needed a support system, and we needed to be able to share without being judged. And we each loved to laugh and enjoy the other's sense of humor. When we agonized over difficult challenges with our children, husbands, or our lives, we could always tell each other, cry openly over a disappointment, or laugh uproariously over something funny. We balanced each other. Sally always "cut to the chase." Sally had an acerbic wit, along with a caring heart. She was never reluctant to tell us when we were either off base or on target. That helped us all immeasurably. Elaine was a cup half full gal, smart as a whip and a fantastic quilter, artist, craftsperson. She could always console herself with a project when her aging jock-o husband behaved like a jerk or her college age daughters were involved in challenging relationships. Elaine knew how to take care of herself and survive. Betty and I watched and learned, and provided solace when appropriate. In so many ways, we were the lucky ones of the four, but being younger, we still had our own hurdles to leap.

For a long time after we left Wilton, we stayed in close touch. Sally was divorced by then, sadly, no surprise. She moved back to northern Ohio where she and I were able to meet for lunch when I traveled from Virginia to visit my aging mama. Sally's divorce was devastating for her, her health suffered, but as always, she was her same quick witted and wonderful self whenever we were together. We talked on the phone occasionally and always held onto our meaningful Wilton connection. How sad I was when her youngest daughter called me ten years ago to say that Sally was found dead in her apartment. I will miss her always. And then, last week, a thoughtful printed letter arrived from Elaine's four daughters, announcing that Elaine died shortly before Christmas this past year. Her seventy-five year-old husband had been killed several years ago in a freakish bogey board accident in the Outer Banks, after which Elaine's health diminished, and her daughters moved her to an assisted living facility. When she died, her oldest daughter sent me a dear note thanking me for a tribute I wrote about Elaine. In it, Kim referred to her mother, Sally, Betty, and me as the "YaYa Sisterhood." While we did not grow up together as children, we certainly matured together as adults. I could hardly wait to tell Betty what Kim said. Being the only official southerner of the four of us, BB, too, loved the reference to "YaYa." So, now only Betty and I remain. We stay in close touch, we see each other with our husbands about once a year; and we email jokes and talk on the phone. We both realize how special our four-way friendship was...and we treasure our memories and the lessons learned from Sally and Elaine. We know the clock is ticking for us, so we welcome opportunities to keep our friendship with each other vibrant. I am reminded of Samuel Johnson's cogent words: *"The endearing elegance of female friendship."*

The other day I found a book tucked into a remote corner of our bookshelves called *The Lost Art of Listening* by Michael P. Nichols, PhD. As I flipped through the pages, many sentences and paragraphs were underlined. What a marvelous treasure this book is! To unearth it at this stage of life makes it even more special. Why is it so important? It is valuable because this book underscores the need for each of us to become astute listeners. Easy, you say? No, not so easy. Why? Most of us like to talk; most of us like to be heard. We think we have wisdom that should be shared. But who of us likes to have someone leap into the middle of a conversation; who of us likes to be interrupted when we really want to finish our thought and just be heard? I know personally how hard I must guard against that habit. Injecting oneself is not becoming, and to hear someone else's experience at a time when we want to be heard is annoying. We may pretend it is okay, but it really is not. Someone who insists upon his own way in a conversation is ultimately perceived as insecure and unable to relinquish the limelight. Not a becoming trait, and certainly not one that will invite intimacy.

"The act of listening requires a submersion of the self and immersion in the other. This isn't always easy. We may be interested but too concerned with controlling or instructing or reforming the other person to be truly open to his point of view."

A good message for each of us pertains to "moving beyond assumptions to openness and empathy: "Shared *thoughts and feelings are a step toward each other. Empathy is the bridge."* To be a good listener, we must honestly care. We must want to hear what is being told to us. That triggers understanding and empathy. It becomes automatic, and the doors to a real friendship swing wide open.

When John and I lived in our First Happy Ever After 'Til the Nursing Home house in Virginia, we were delighted to learn that another corporate couple our age planned to build a house down the long driveway from us. We were delighted. One day, as I was walking Martha, our dog, a car pulled up, the driver's window rolled down, and inside were our future neighbors, Debbie and Ron. Excited to welcome them to our rural neighborhood, I invited them to our house for a cup of coffee. They accepted most graciously, and thus the genesis of a wonderful close relationship. For the last twenty-four years, Debbie and Ron, John and I have shared happy and sad times. We have weathered retirement, moved to other homes, welcomed each other's grandchildren, and now great grandchildren, and supported each other's medical crises. We have grown rich from each other's strong spirits. We care about each other deeply.

So, when Deb and Ron decided to move away from our road to another house, we were sad. Although understanding their rationale, I remember feeling upset and disappointed because they had the audacity to sell their house. WHO were the new people? Would we have anything at all in common, or would we just nod politely at each other as we walked out to get our mail? Although I remained skeptical, Debbie assured me that we would like the new owners. Common sense prevailed, and I decided that we needed to invite the new couple to supper with Deb and Ron. I will never forget that evening. Linda and Rich arrived, gracious as can be, and it wasn't long before I said to Linda, "I need to tell you it is going to be hard for me to have Debbie and Ron leave, and to see you living in their house." Boy, was I blunt, but truthful! Talk about a good listener...Linda immediately soothed me with her kindness, and her words, "I don't blame you one bit, I would feel exactly the same way if I were you." What a lady, what a generous response to an insensitive comment by me. I knew then that Linda was going to become a part of my life. And the rest is history.

As a result, many years later, Debbie, Linda, and I have become quite close friends, gathering as often as possible at Brio's for lunch, long lingering lunches, that often extend from 12:30 p.m. to nearly 4 p.m.. We ask to be seated on the same side of the restaurant where noise is minimal, we always order the same salads, and have dubbed ourselves The Brio Trio. The beauty of this three-way friendship is that we open ourselves up to in-depth discussions. As Linda says, we "start with hair, then books and movies," and move on from there to many personal issues. Listening to each other is easy, and learning from each other always happens. To think that three women, two in their seventies and one in her sixties, from different areas of the country with different political and religious beliefs, different degrees of education can interact on such a unique level is quite amazing. Linda, the youngest, has a PhD in physiology. She is a full professor at the Medical College of Virginia (VCU), a retired associate dean. She is a well known (published in several languages) text book author, and a brilliant, humble and lovely lady. Debbie is younger than I by six months, and her faith is immutable. Her religion is a small fundamental sect, and her beliefs are solidly biblically based. She is the mother of three, the wife of a former corporate executive, and the survivor of a difficult childhood. Debbie is innately bright, well read and the epitome of patience and understanding. We resonate with each other. And when John had sepsis, these ladies were at the hospital nearly every day sitting in the waiting room while I was with John. This unique friendship began quite by accident, for if we three had not chosen to live on a little road tucked into the woods of Goochland County, Virginia, we would never have met. Our paths probably would not have crossed, but thank God they did.

Do we ever have "sticky" moments with our friends? I suppose there are, but nothing significant with really close friends. The reason is that communication is fluid, and communication allows us to say, "Gosh, I shouldn't have said that." We admit a mistake, give an apology, and move forward. Debbie recently said to me (after an email exchange about years-old yarn she found, and I said, "Dump it or give it to the Salvation Army,") "Joy, you don't need to apologize to me for saying that." Well, I worried I had overstepped my bounds. I did, but because Debbie is the incredible person and close friend she is, she dismissed it, and never let me feel guilty for my inadvertent words. Thus, no stickiness!

On the other hand, there was a couple in Connecticut whom we met through corporate life. John and I gradually became connected to them. We skied in Vermont, they came for a visit to Virginia, and we had fun. They

153

were nice people. They even came to our older son's wedding. As parents of two daughters who married later in life, they were delighted when their first daughter became engaged. We knew we would be invited to the wedding, which was to be a lavish affair. While we didn't really know the daughter, we felt obligated to attend because of her parents. Little did we realize until the invitation arrived that we would be out of the country. I promptly wrote our sincere regrets and explained John's unexpected business trip to Paris. We sent a lovely gift, in hopes of compensating for our failure to attend. When we returned from abroad, I called to hear about the wedding. When my "friend" answered the phone, and heard who I was, she said, "I don't have anything to say to you." Oh my goodness. I could not believe my ears. I tried to explain, I tried to make this woman understand, but anything I said, or anything I did to make amends fell on deaf ears. The friendship was over, and I shot it dead as a doornail. I felt horrible. But there was nothing I could do. I had to accept that this once meaningful (to me) friendship was built on sand, with nothing to undergird it. That was the end of it, pure and simple. John listened to the long story, but said he was not surprised by this lady's reaction. To say that I learned from this experience is an understatement. I learned that if a friendship dissolves over something shallow, then it was not a friendship of any consequence. Thank heavens, this has never happened to us again. Amen. Time to move on.

As great as it is to have friends of our own age and stage of life, it is always fun to have younger ones, too. I call a few of these cute gals my "adopted daughters" and tell then that because our two daughters and daughters-in-law live so far away, I need to "borrow" them now and then for a "daughter fix!" How refreshing to spend time with one of my favorite young friends...I love it that they seem happy to spend this time together, too. The fun thing is that I haven't forgotten what it felt like to be a fifty something year-old. As I spend time with these women, I try to develop better listening skills. Also, important for this old girl to watch for Duct Tape moments. It is a good exercise. We all know how important it is to slap on the Duct Tape with our own families.

Perhaps one of the hardest aspects of contemplating the move to a retirement facility is the truism that *everyone will be older.* Now I understand why when we were much younger, neighbors would occasionally comment on having a young family living on the street. It is good to "shake us up." It is good to mix up the generations, so that none of us becomes stale and stagnant. It is good for everyone. It is good to hear other points of view from different age perspectives. It keeps us on our toes. God forbid people of my generation should morph into being boring old folks. But when the time comes to move to the retirement facility, then we are charged with the mission to find a way to keep ourselves in touch with the younger generations….to keep our ears open to what they are saying, and to allow ourselves interaction with youth. This will be hardest for those of us whose families are far flung. Thus, we must consciously seek out those younger people whom we can "borrow" for a short time, interact with, and enjoy. They can be our friends, too.

Someone once told me that if you can count your closest friends on one hand, you are lucky. I think that as we age and as we continue to remain vibrant, it is possible to count them on both hands and maybe even a few toes. The delight of accumulating and keeping precious friends as long as we each live is overwhelmingly satisfying. Some of us need more friends than others do, and some of us are more naturally outgoing. But no matter our personality, we know that a beloved friend fills a void in our hearts. I think about the future, when we move to a retirement home. Friendships will definitely matter. I doubt anyone wants to move to a place where they know no one. However, some people have no choice, and many do well. Some move away from their homes to a new area where their children live. That takes courage, but it can make enormous good sense.

I remember Sarah M. who decided at age eighty it was the "right time" to sell her house in South Carolina, and move to Richmond, to a retirement home. She chose Virginia because it was where her only daughter Sally and family lived. Sarah was spunky. She made up her mind to adjust, even though she left many good friends behind. She was remarkable, she was consummately gracious, and she was and is my role model for accepting change late in life. I will always be grateful for Sarah's example. At age seventy-seven, I think of her often, and remind myself that she moved well and adjusted beautifully. It was not long before Sarah became well acquainted with the other ladies who lived at Westminster Canterbury. Having her daughter and family close by eased the transition and whatever loneliness she felt. But they had their lives, and they could not see Sarah on a daily basis. Her efforts to be absorbed into the fabric of retirement life were laudable and they were rewarded. She was a delight to everyone. As time passed, Sarah's health declined, but never her optimistic point of view. She lived a long life, well into her nineties, and she died knowing that by moving to a retirement home in Richmond, Sarah had done everything she could to minimize becoming a burden on her daughter's life. This kind of selflessness is special. My guess is that even at her advanced age, Sarah reached out and made good friends. She allowed herself to be a good friend, too. She shared her joy.

Treasured quotes from Ralph Waldo Emerson:

> *"A friend is a person with whom I may be sincere. Before him, I may think aloud."*
> *"A friend may well be reckoned the masterpiece of Nature."*
> *"The only reward of virtue is virtue; the only way to have a friend is to be a friend."*

Living the Cup Half Full Life

Living the cup half full life is a mindset that benefits each of us all our lives. The older we grow, the more important it becomes to practice this daily. We all know people who are always cheery, and we know those who are not. My grandmother was a miserable old lady, and as a little girl, I remember wanting to run from her. She was picky about everything, she never smiled, and it always upset me that she was cross with my mother. Grandma obsessed about her aches and pains, and she complained about every aspect of her own life. How sad. Of course she had a difficult time when she and my grandfather were divorced after my mother and aunt were married. In those pre-Depression days, divorce was quite unusual. And perhaps that is one reason my grandmother became so cranky, difficult, and mean. No matter what, I learned early on that the last thing I wanted to be when I grew up and old was a crotchety old lady. I wanted my children and grandchildren to *want* to be around me, and it was up to me to decide if they would or would not. Interesting how early children can make conscious decisions for themselves and their futures.

Taped to the cupboard over my computer is a wonderful, dog-eared piece of paper. I have had it for several years, and it says:

ATTITUDE

"ATTITUDE, to me, is more important than facts, than the past, than education, than money, than circumstances, than failures, than successes, than what other people say, think or do.

It is more important than appearance, giftedness or skill. It will make or break a company, family relationship or home.

The remarkable thing is that we have a choice every morning regarding the attitude we will embrace that day.

We can't change the past.

We can't change the fact people will act in a certain way.

We can't change the inevitable.

The only thing we can do is play the one card we have.

And that is attitude.

I am convinced that life is 10% what happens and 90% how I handle it."

Reading this yet again confirms why I like it so much. Just as my grandmother could not see anything positive in her life, so too is it sad that no one bothered to help her figure out why she felt as she did. A divorce in itself could not have tilted her perspective to such a degree, because it would seem that perhaps her "attitude" contributed to the unhappiness of that marriage. Not for me to say, as I do not know, nor do I believe my mother did either. In those days, people were supposed to live their lives, and go forward as best as they could. Professional help for anxiety or depression was not an option unless it was medically necessary.

For retirees whose lives are suddenly or dramatically altered it is a blessing that today's world encourages people to seek help. Some people who are stressed, or who find themselves struggling with the changes, are able to work through each hurdle by themselves. Maybe this is their personality, maybe it is their attitude, and maybe it is prior life experience. But in any event, it is quite comforting that in today's world *no one* need be saddled with the yoke of emotional dysfunction. We have talked about this in a previous section, but it is worth repeating so as to keep the message alive. A visit to one's primary care physician can open the door to professional help. A person can be given a prescription to relieve anxiety or depression, and a PC doctor is often equipped to refer his or her patient to a trained psychotherapist or psychologist. And best of all, there is no stigma associated with it.

I look at our two plucky daughters who survived multiple moves with their father and me, and I applaud their upbeat attitudes, even when times are difficult. They each claim that moving did not bother them. "It was our way of life." How brave and kind of them to say that, but deep down they must have felt like rubber balls, bouncing from one school, one new town and playground to another. How hard it must have been to make friends, find good playmates, only to leave them and start all over again. My girls were and are special human beings. They are both in their fifties, although each one will never be that old in my book. (After all, I am way too young to have such old kids!) Each one is supportive of a husband whose needs are far different than their father's were. Allison has been her family's breadwinner for many of her married years. She has managed also to leave her boys with no college debt and be a wonderful mother. Living in urban Boston, she credits much of her adult sons' well being to their father who was often available to the boys. Negativity is not part of Allison's personality, and she is her family's constant cheerleader.

Just as Allison has done her best to juggle a demanding career and family, so, too, has Susie held her family "forever in the palm of her hand." To supplement their income, she has worked far more years than she has been a stay-at-home mom. Although an excellent executive secretary she realized early on she did not want her children raised in a daycare system. She left corporate life with its demands, and taught pre-school as her daughter and son grew up. Now she is an administrative assistant for her large Christian church where her skills and engaging personality are highly valued. Both children are seniors, one in college and one in high school. Susie's priority has been to be available to them, and soon, when Brad leaves for college, she can reenter the more competitive corporate environment, if she chooses. As we all know, the job market is not easy, and recently Susie's CPA husband, along with many, many other Microsoft employees, was downsized. In the last year, three of our four adult children have suffered job loss: Allison, whose beloved private equity company succumbed to a difficult economy, was quickly hired by another retail firm, and Charley, with a generous severance, was employed by another large corporation before his package expired. And now Brent, our Seattle CPA son-in-law's protracted search has ended. He received two job offers in two days. He says that these many anxious months have taught him a powerful lesson: in today's economic climate, one must always remain an active networker. He or she must keep eyes and options open. How gratifying to see these younger generations respond with a positive attitude. They believe they can manage any obstacle that arises: we old folks realize that approach to life builds character! (A wonderful book to read is David Brooks, *The Road to Character.* No matter your age, you will walk away with renewed wisdom and determination to try harder to be a better person: one whose willingness to learn and grow as a human being is lifelong. Thank you, David Brooks.)

Being a daughter-in-law who is a licensed pediatric neuro-psychologist as well as the daughter of a trained psychotherapist, Stephanie is tuned into the signals that emanate from someone needing help. It is a comfort to run things by her, not frequently but when the situation merits. She has a wonderful way of being professional with her family, yet mindful of the broader picture. I am sure that even as a student she had skilled instincts, and during the early years of John's retirement, she and I had some wonderful chats. We still do, but often about many other topics. At least as a corporate wife talking to a former corporate wife, she can ask me questions about rigors of being married to a man working for big business. Sometimes, I offer opinions when asked, other times I don't but at least she always seems glad to know what I think. She *knows* I respect her expertise, and benefit by it.

One can even say that Living the Cup Half Full life transcends many of today's marriages. While there are still the traditional couples where the husband works and the wife stays home, some women have high powered jobs, some men are home, and neither partner feels stuck in one roll. How different it was when John and I were young. Women of my generation remember when, if ever, daddy bathed the children, washed the dishes, did a load of laundry. Now, many husbands come home from work, roll up their sleeves, and help their wives with household chores and children. This is a common practice. I love seeing our sons empty dishwashers, fold laundry, cook, and help their wives. That is healthy sharing, if you ask me. Because Sam's office is in the same town where he and his wife and daughters live, he can fill in gaps with the girls when needed. He loves having solo time to interact with all three daughters. While Allison is the family breadwinner, she says her husband does all the grocery shopping, vacuuming, and laundry. She cooks but finds it is "therapy" after a long day. Susie's husband Brent keeps a Master Gardner yard, where never a twig or a leaf falls unnoticed. His attention to detail is unequalled, and every flower, every bush could be featured in a magazine. He may not do housework, but his garage is organized and immaculate. Four years ago, when Stephanie decided to resume her career, to push forward before her existing preliminary credentials became invalid, she and Charley filled their marital cup up to the rim as they adapted a new way of life. Even after a full day of corporate demands, he willingly assumed numerous household tasks plus those related to raising their two daughters. Demands on both Stephanie and Charley were heavy, but they worked it out. Steph reached her goal, secured a part-time staff position at the University of Arkansas, and Charley discovered that making dinner in addition to working a full corporate day was creative and interesting, rather than an ordeal. He loves to cook. They have achieved a successful partnership, as have many other modern young couples negotiating a double income family.

Our other daughter-in-law Joan sets a shining example for her and Sam's three girls and actually also for those of us at any age who may face medical problems, big or small. "Good things come in small packages" is what Sam first said about his Joan. She stretches on her tippy toes to stand five feet tall. As a young child of five or six she endured the painful divorce of her parents, but she was richly blessed by her mother's happy marriage to her wonderful stepfather. She has had numerous surgeries, including three C-sections, yet she never falters, she never complains, and she is always looking at "the bright side." I love her approach to any problem. She tackles it head on, does what is necessary to solve it, and moves forward. When she broke her wrist while running on a remote Connecticut country road several years ago, she realized she had left her cell phone in her car. She was in the middle of no-where. There were no houses, zero car traffic. The only way to get help was to find it. Wow! She did. Limping two or three miles back to her car, she did not go into shock, and she drove herself to safety. Her badly broken wrist required not one, but a second surgery. She is a model of courage and no-nonsense for her girls, so much so that when at age nine, Abigail, the youngest and a budding gymnast, fell from the parallel bars and broke her arm in several places, she was able to look at her mommy in the ER and say, "Don't worry, mom, these things happen to athletes!" Although she isn't even fifty, my guess is that Joan will always be a Cup Half Full girl.

Having received an unexpected change of address card and personal note recently from a Mobile, Alabama friend, I picked up the phone and reconnected with the ninety-three year-old grandmother of sixteen and great grandmother of sixteen. We moved from Mobile in 1976, and I have only seen Joyce once or twice since. Talking to her was a delight. We had not been in touch for several years, but for her to remember us and to reach out to John and me was not only a surprise but also a delight. When we moved to Mobile in 1974, this lady was the first corporate wife to call and invite me to lunch. In spite of our age difference, we became friends, and I never forgot her graciousness or her generosity. She was the epitome of southern hospitality. And we enjoyed many happy adventures together. Although she lost her wonderful husband fifteen years ago, both of her sons, and numerous young relatives to cancer, she radiates optimism and the "cup half full" attitude. As she said over the phone, "I will be fine, Joy, as long as my mind doesn't abandon me. I won't mind living to one hundred if I can still think clearly and be alert." And so far, she is still driving, with limitations imposed by her family, although not the six to eight hour drives of yore. Reconnecting with this remarkable lady reminded me of the importance once more of reaching out, as she did. At age ninety-three, she showed me that our lives weave many threads. Some are stronger than others, but they are tight, if we hold on to them, and loose only if we choose.

Keeping the "cup half full" has its difficult moments. As we have said, there are inevitable bumps during retirement. Our status can morph and change each day. My first dear Richmond friend Sally, widowed two years ago, introduced the "new normal" phrase to me during the period when she and her brave husband were battling his insurmountable medical problems. And to think that Gary's poor health struck just as he retired from his dedicated and successful periodontal practice. The coincidence underscores the sadness of the situation. He and Sally never had a chance to enjoy what so many of us are blessed to have. Although they had the "wherewithal," they never had the luxury to do as they pleased, the time to travel together, and freedom to embrace the beauty of their new chapter in life.

We older people realize that age alters many aspects of our lives. They are subtle changes. They sneak up on us, but they do occur. Sometimes we wish we could go back twenty or thirty years. Sometimes we yearn for our old vitality and energy. But, if we have our health, security, and are able to think straight, we must give ourselves permission to appreciate our blessings more each day. Our love for our spouses becomes more precious. In our youth we could hardly wait to jump under the sheets to express our love for each other. But now, life is different. We show our love in so many wonderful ways...maybe by realizing intuitively what the other one is feeling or thinking. Maybe by laughing at the same movie, or reacting the same to a news bulletin from TV or family. We cannot begin to count the ways that we feel our long enduring love. We express our love with a look, a pat, a hug or a cuddle. We cannot begin to take for granted the incredible luxury of waking up next to the person who makes our heart sing, even when he snores or takes all the covers over to his side of the bed! Count our blessings each and every day. I love Martin Luther's words written in the fifteenth or sixteenth century: *"There is no more lovely, friendly and charming relationship, communion or company than a good marriage."* Centuries later, his words continue to ring true.

One day when we were talking on the phone, Sally said that each medical situation she and Gary encountered created a "new normal" for them. Ever since she said that, I have realized how apropos it is of all aspects of our later years. Everything keeps evolving. I realize that as time passes, it is just as important to embrace change as another of life's adventures as it is to keep our minds and hearts open. In five years of constant decline, countless hospital stays, one can never remember when Sally or Gary, as sick as he was, did not drink of that "cup half full." He never lost his cute sense of humor, his interest in others, or his appreciation for the quality, limited though it became, of his and Sally's life together. Their inspiration to all around them, family, friends, doctors, and nurses, was monumental. Perhaps one reason they were so positive, so upbeat even when Sally was sleeping in ICU at the hospital or managing Gary's pic line at home, was because of their strong faith as well as their beautiful, loving marriage. They were also blessed to have a host of friends, two married children in the same city, and two others who could often come as needed. The day of Gary's memorial service was a celebration not only of his incredible life, but of one couple's eternal belief that "we can manage anything" that comes our way. As Winston Churchill once said, *"A pessimist sees the difficulty in every opportunity. An optimist sees the opportunity in every difficulty."*

If I were to enumerate the lessons learned over the last seventeen years of retirement they would fill another book. The most important truth is that each day I witness something more that I want to embrace. John is a great example for me. I love how my husband maintains his quick sense of humor. I know he wishes I would stop reminding him to comb his hair, hike up his drooping trousers, or cut his nose hairs, but he is always able to diffuse my suggestions with a joke. I love how he and some of his friends banter together, over their golf scores, or their poor shots, or their declining mobility. They have learned the importance of laughing at themselves. John teaches me every day. And I know deep in my psyche how important it is for me to strive always to be a better person: to be more thoughtful, more loving, less critical, more encouraging, more understanding, and more aware of how lucky I am to be on this earth. Sometimes a fresh insight pops into my mind.... when I least expect it. I want to fight against negativity. I want to see the truth as it presents itself clearly, but I want to be able to share it only when asked. I don't want to dismiss a new idea just because it is out of my comfort zone. That can be a trap for so many older people. Sometimes I say to myself, "why didn't you do it this way, or why didn't you give more of yourself to someone you love or admire who is struggling? Why don't you put your own needs on the back burner and concentrate on someone else's?" John says I am too critical of myself, but I reply that if I am unaware of my faults, how can I cure them? We only have one shot at this life, and we can't ignore an opportunity to learn and grow. As Luc De Clapiers wrote in the eighteenth century, *"The things we know best are the things we have not learned."*

When we seniors contemplate what we have learned during our lives we know we have compiled a wealth of knowledge. Some is meaningful, and some is useless. For me, as a late in life writer, I believe the only worthwhile wisdom I am equipped to share pertains to experiences I have lived, people I have known or know, and lessons that are embedded in my heart. It is shallow, meaningless, and invalid to pretend to know anything else. Try as we might, we can't fool anyone with false information. People with insight see right through us. Lessons learned can be shared, but it is up to those who hear or read them to decide for themselves what they choose to retain. I believe that goodness prevails, that in the last analysis, truth is ultimate. I believe we can each be whomever we want to be. We can impact those whose lives we touch, and we can make a difference in a small or large way. Why else is it that each of us often harkens back to lessons taught by parents or loved ones who are long gone? Why else is it that we find ourselves quoting their words? And why is it that our memories retain all these thoughts? Because they made a difference to us, and they matter. They helped shape us as people. They impacted us, our way of living and our attitude toward others. Our task is to "pay it forward."

For those of you who remember the story of Pollyanna, this sounds like a "goodie two shoes" approach to life. No one can be perfect, no one can be all things to all people, no one can give one hundred percent of himself or herself to others. Pollyanna is a children's story, told to accentuate the lesson to be a "good" person who views life as cheery, positive, and the cup half full. My goal is to maximize the gifts that God has given me. As a little girl, I remember constant reminders by my mother, "Remember, your name is Joy!" And once, I even recall feeling a resounding kick under the dining room table when she caught me pouting. No way was that allowed in our house. What a gift my mother gave me. Being named "Joy" is a responsibility, and one I want to try to fulfill.

Living in a world fraught with turmoil as we all do, it is even more important to give as much of ourselves to others as we can. We all know those whose lives have been cruelly affected by death, disease, divorce, financial reversal, or just plain bad luck. We never know when something devastating will happen to our loved ones or us. We don't know if our world will stay together for another generation, or whether our children and grandchildren will have the lifelong joys that we have been given. But we do know that with the grace of God and the providence of reasonable health we can be the people we want to be. We can take charge of ourselves for as long as possible. We can keep our eyes and our ears open, we can learn from history and from those whose stories reveal unexpected truths.

Reading the book by David McCullough about the Wright Brothers reminded me of the basic values espoused by my parents who were toddlers when Orville and Wilbur flew their first "aero plane." These brothers, for all of their creative and intellectual brilliance, reflected, among other things, faith in God, modesty, patience, appreciation, gentleness, determination, and tolerance for those who did not understand their passion to create a "flying machine." As we live in our modern world often dominated by sporadic terrorism locally and internationally, divisive politics, cyber bullying, social media gone awry, let's pause to revisit the people who made our country great: a place of unequaled opportunity and advantage. Let's read the heartwarming stories of everyday valor often super-ceded by sensationalist news; let's view life through a positive lens rather than a negative one. Let's treat each other with respect, ever mindful of "unto thine own self be true," and let's never be satisfied with mediocrity.

If religion is important in our lives, let us also increase and lean on our faith in God. When John and I skip church on a summer Sunday because we decide to sit on our porch and be quiet, we read devotions to each other. We read from the Psalms, from Dietrich Bonhoeffer's daily devotions called *I Want to Live These Days with You.* The prose is wonderful, inspiring and strong, as was Bonheoffer, who was a brilliant and valiant German Christian theologian prisoner hung by the Nazis on the last day of World War II in 1945. There is another book given to John by a retired doctor friend that we love called *Voices from the Past,* which contains many Puritan writings. An excerpt that particularly resonates at this time of our lives is: God *"is directing you to eternal life and by his counsel. He is leading you to the world of light where there are rivers of pleasure and fullness of joy forever more. There you will see his face and feel his love. Is not such a guide desirable?"* Reading these words make us unafraid of the future, what lies ahead, and be reassured that we will be just fine, no matter what happens. May we all feel so blessed.

Like each of you, I care deeply about those I love and like: about their lives, their worries and their challenges. I want each one to realize how much they are valued, how much they are appreciated, and how special they are in my heart. Each of our lives is an hourglass. Sand falls steadily to the bottom, signaling that life is running away from us. I have learned that at any time, when we least expect it, something earth shattering can happen... whether it be a fall, a medical event, or a loss of monumental proportions. This accelerates the need to maximize the time left in as positive a way as possible. I have learned, especially since my traumatic carotid episode and John's sepsis near death scare to appreciate each good day. We cannot take our well-being or that of our loved ones for granted. I want to be a giving person, not someone who sits back waiting to see what others will do for me. I want to keep striving to be a better person, I want to work on my deficiencies so that as the sand continues to sift downward, I won't look back and have too many regrets. I hope and pray that I can live the life "half full" all the rest of my days.

Poor Grandma Effie who cast unhappy shadows all around her. What a shame for others, but mostly for herself. She died in her early eighties, but to me in my youthful naivety, she was never anything but a sad and pitiful old lady. Yet, the one thing she did do that everyone appreciated was to make incredibly beautiful aprons and embroidered monogramed pillowcases. Her handwork, her stitches, her creativity jumped off of each piece. And gradually I have come to realize that her gift of love, disguised though it was by her in person, was sewn into her handiwork. Too bad I wasn't old enough or wise enough then to realize that. I wish I could tell her now that I am sorry not to have been a loving granddaughter, a more understanding one. I can't, but I can try to keep my cup *always* half full... Oh yes, we all evolve, some of us more slowly than others, but before the breath goes out in our bodies, let us never forget that inside most every soul there is something of value, something that may lie dormant until the right time for it to be revealed. *"Life just gives us time and space, it is up to us to fill it."* Or as Nelson Mandela writes, *"As we let our own light shine, we unconsciously give other people permission to do the same."* Help spread the joy of being alive, and celebrate the Joy of Retirement!

$\mathcal{A}$cknowledgements

What began as a project to assuage winter doldrums and a tenacious respiratory infection has morphed into one of the most delightful nine months of my life. It has generated far fewer labor pains than giving birth, but hopefully it has produced helpful stories and observations that can assist others in their journey through retirement years. Writing this book has allowed me to plumb experiences of the past and the present and caused me to address the future with all of its unknown challenges. Writing this book has offered me the opportunity to look at our lives on earth as a scientist might observe a petri dish. We take one day at a time, but we never lose sight of the need to be prepared for what lies ahead. I am grateful to all those relatives and friends who took the time to read chapters throughout their metamorphoses, to offer suggestions, comments and additional reading material for me to ponder.

Those people who deserve extra special thanks are a wonderful book agent friend from Connecticut named Denise Marcil, who thoughtfully introduced me to amazing and supportive editor/publisher/author Charlene Giannetti of WAT-AGE Publishing LLC. She agreed to take me as a client. Her wisdom has expanded my thinking, and her willingness to promote this late-in-life author is a blessing of monumental proportions! In addition, Charlene has become a wonderful friend whom I will revere always.

Reading a manuscript as it evolves is not always an easy task. Two people in addition to Charlene Giannetti warrant my eternal appreciation. Because of the astute observations of my deeply admired friend Dr. Linda Costanzo, author of several college text books and profession of physiology at Virginia Commonwealth University, and my bright Wellesley College English major sister Judy Goetz, I was able to grow along with the book. Judy exhausted many print cartridges as she copied ongoing versions of this book. Her insights were great, and she also recommended the manuscript to her Arizona condo friend Martha Updike, author John Updike's widow and once my childhood playmate. Because of you all, this book and its author thrived.

To those friends and family members who read *JOY* in its infancy and toddlerhood, big hugs! To my cousin Robin Mayer and friends Dr. Ron Barton, Elizabeth Bradley, Delle Jones, Debbie McPhee, Dr. Harriss Ricks, Jr., Linda Seifert, Marion Touchette and Martha Updike as well as my chicks Allison McCabe and Sam Nevin, Charley Nevin and daughter in-law Joan Nevin, mega thanks for offering your honest, helpful and forthright reactions. An extra smooch to daughter Susie Taylor for her awesome design ideas. Taking a slice out of the cake was the perfect touch!

Kudos to our ALL our far flung family: from daughter in-law Stephanie, sons in-law Brent Taylor and Conall McCabe; grandchildren Liam and Natalie McCabe; Seamus, Melody and baby Declan McCabe; Allison and Brad Taylor; Lucy, Caroline and Abigail Nevin; Livvie and Emmy Joy Nevin, my cup overflows. How lucky I am, and how blessed we are to have John Nevin as our Chief Cheerleader! Rah!

Another special hug to Nicolas Pratt, a bona fide Apple Genius, for his many hours of patient tutorial sessions. I am learning slowly, but you make me feel as if all things are possible. Now I understand why so many authors attribute their completed writing to their family and friends. Nothing worthwhile happens by itself, and the more we open our mind to new ideas, thoughts and methods, the more we allow ourselves the gift of evolving as people who Live, Love, and Learn.

A posthumous thanks to William Zinsser, journalist, Yale professor and author of *On Writing Well* and *Writing About your Life*. Reading his books is a vicarious college course in writing. Praise to Dr. Linda Costanzo for introducing me to his works.

To Jai Williams of *Januari Jai Media* in Washington, D.C., a talented photographer, whose gentle patience and consummate love of her work translates into a glorious experience of time with her and pictures made by her. Wishing her a beautiful future with hugs and thanks from "Miss Joy."

To *Desserterie Bakery* of Midlothian, Virginia, your cake tastes just as delicious as it looks. Please know I extend joyful gratitude to the bakery's staff for creating an exquisite confection inside and outside.

How exciting to realize that at age seventy-seven one can be consumed with a new passion: one that won't require anything but a comfy chair, a working computer, a window to the outdoors, and a quiet spot to sort, select and think. My prayer is that we can keep this conversation going, and I will have the chance to write about the final chapter of life once we make the move to our retirement home. Therein lies a whole new treasure trove of adventures!

Joy Nevin was born and raised in Cleveland, Ohio, graduated from Hathaway Brown School and attended Connecticut College (for Women) in New London, Connecticut. She has been married to John Nevin for 58 years, is the mother of four married children, grandmother of nine, and great-grandmother of one. Her first book, *GET MOVING:A Joyful Search to Meet and Embrace Life Transitions* was published in 2002. She and her husband have moved more than a dozen times and are happily settled in Manakin Sabot, Virginia.